Samuel Miner Campbell

Across the Desert

A Life of Moses

Samuel Miner Campbell

Across the Desert
A Life of Moses

ISBN/EAN: 9783743312463

Manufactured in Europe, USA, Canada, Australia, Japa

Cover: Foto ©Lupo / pixelio.de

Manufactured and distributed by brebook publishing software (www.brebook.com)

Samuel Miner Campbell

Across the Desert

ACROSS THE DESERT.

A LIFE OF MOSES.

BY THE
REV. S. M. CAMPBELL, D.D.

WITH MAPS AND ILLUSTRATIONS.

PHILADELPHIA:
PRESBYTERIAN BOARD OF PUBLICATION,
No. 1334 CHESTNUT STREET.

Entered according to Act of Congress, in the year 1873, by
THE TRUSTEES OF THE
PRESBYTERIAN BOARD OF PUBLICATION,
In the Office of the Librarian of Congress, at Washington.

WESTCOTT & THOMSON,
Stereotypers and Electrotypers, Philada.

SHERMAN & CO.,
Printers, Philada.

PREFACE.

What the apostle Paul was to the Christian Church, that Moses was before him to the Church of the Old Testament times. The world needs a life of Moses corresponding in some good degree to the great work of Conybeare and Howson on the life of the apostle Paul.

While we are waiting for such a production, however, it may be that a volume of smaller proportions and of less scholarly pretensions would be of service. For Sabbath-school teachers, for ministers and for all who study the Scriptures, a condensed, consecutive, carefully-prepared account of the incidents of Moses' life is much to be desired.

His own need of such a work has led the author to make the present venture. What he wanted he believed might be of use to others;

and as a man who cannot find the house which he wants ready made, must need build one if he be able, he has carefully sought out such material as was accessible and arranged it in this volume. It is scarcely a palace that has grown into shape under his hand. To some it will not seem even a cottage. Be it so. A tent will serve for a journey across the desert; and if any one would like to share the shelter with him for a short tour, the author only has to say, "Come in."

After placing the work in the hands of the publishers the author made a somewhat extended journey to the Orient, visiting Egypt and the Holy Land, and on his return he embodied the fruits of his tour in a careful revision of these pages. But not to rest his statements entirely on his own observations, he makes constant reference to accepted authorities in the body of the work. S. M. C.

Rochester, N. Y., July, 1872.

CONTENTS.

I.—WONDER LAND.

A picture of Egypt. How the country was made. Lower Egypt. Goshen. "No rain in Egypt." The Nile. The Pharaohs. The Hyksos. When the bondage began.................... 19

II.—OUTCAST.

The law to destroy the Hebrew children. Birth of Moses. Parentage. His beauty. Hiding the child. The ark of bulrushes. The papyrus. Pitch. The crocodiles.................... 25

III.—PHARAOH'S DAUGHTER.

Nile-bathing. A religious service. In the morning. When the child was put in the ark. Pharaoh's palace. A discovery. A nurse for the child. A mother's care...................... 30

IV.—IN THE HOUSE OF PHARAOH.

A great change for the lad. Wisdom of the Egyptians. Inspiration and study. Mighty words of Moses. Mighty deeds. God can raise up the man for the hour.................... 36

V.—IN THE HOUSE OF BONDAGE.

At work for the king. The treasure cities were fortifications. Pithom and Rameses. The people not slaves. Rash attempt to lead them off. Failure. Flight...................... 42

VI.—IN A STRANGE LAND.

Peninsula of Sinai. The wadys. A dry country. A silent country. Moses' route. Raguel and his daughters. The shepherds. Zipporah. God's plan.. 47

VII.—A VOICE.

Changes in forty years. Raguel and Jethro. The chieftain's home. The acacia tree. The burning bush. The angel. Oriental reverence... 52

VIII.—RELUCTANCE.

"Coming down." A hard commission. God's name. The first asking. Slow speech. An unwilling man. Aaron to help. Aaron ready... 59

IX.—DOWN FROM THE DESERT.

Entering upon duty. Release from Jethro. The infant sons. Moses' sons not conspicuous men. The rod of God. A great misadventure. The inn. Without his family. Aaron.......... 63

X.—BEGINNING AGAIN.

Now and forty years ago. Hebrew national organization. The patriarchal system. The elders. First assembly. Two miracles. All promises well.. 69

XI.—HOW IT STRIKES THE KING.

What Pharaoh knows of Moses. The first interview. A modest request. How it was enforced. Who is the Lord? A failure.. 72

CONTENTS.

XII.—WORSE AND WORSE.

Brickmaking. The pyramids. Need of straw in making brick. Grim humor. Brick without straw. Taskmasters and officers. Complaining to the king. Reproaches of the people. Moses' talk with God.. 75

XIII.—THE MYSTERIOUS NAME.

Names of gods. Hebrew God no proper name. Parentage of the gods. I Am. Jehovah. Name not previously assumed. The veneration felt for the word. Jehovah-Jesus................. 84

XIV.—SENT ONCE MORE.

A former scene repeated. The covenant. Objections answered. Pharaoh again. A miracle demanded. The magicians. Legerdemain. Hardening his heart. How it was done............ 89

XV.—THE TWO RIVER PLAGUES.

Skirmishing. Battle. Two by two. A word and a blow. A It hurled at the Nile-god. Pharaoh's plan to sustain himself. The frogs. Nervous terror. The first promise............ 95

XVI.—THE TWO INSECT PLAGUES.

Smiting the gods and subduing Pharaoh. Beetles and gnats. The Hebrews safe. Magicians fail. A new promise. Sacred animals. The abominations of the Egyptians..................... 101

XVII.—THE PLAGUES OF PESTILENCE.

The old formula. God's hand on the cattle. The cattle in Goshen. Cattle gods. The plague on the priestly caste. Remonstrance with the king. His stubborn impiety 108

XVIII.—THE PLAGUES ON THE FRUITS OF THE EARTH.

Sacred plants. A heathen god and the Christian God. The Egyptian religion fetichism. Hail. Good men at the palace. Time of year. The locusts. Emancipation. A controversy and a promise...... 112

XIX.—DARKNESS AND DEATH.

The crisis approaching. Clear sky in Egypt. Dry air. The plagues of darkness and dampness. The king's proposal rejected. Light in the Hebrew dwellings. Preparation. Death...... 123

XX.—MAKING READY.

Moving great bodies of men. Details arranged. Borrowing the jewels. Passover. In-doors. The lamb. The blood. Christ our passover. The "two evenings." Waiting. It comes...... 129

XXI.—FORWARD.

The 430 years. Possible increase of population. Free to go. Place of starting. The mixed multitude. The kneading-troughs. Harnessed. The pillar of fire. Succoth...... 138

XXII.—PURSUIT.

Change of scenery. Etham. Desert features. The third day out. A new order. Pharaoh's scouts. His military force. Gulf of Suez. Jebel Attaka. A trap...... 146

XXIII.—A NIGHT TO BE REMEMBERED.

The terrible chariots. Bad behavior. Dignity of Moses. "A light to these and darkness to those." Storm. Through the sea. How he dare follow. Daylight. Route. Zoan. Low tide...... 156

CONTENTS.

XXIV.—THE GREAT AND TERRIBLE DESERT.

Geological formation. Lebanon to Sinai. The core of the peninsula. Wadys, drought, springs, reservoirs. Denudation of the desert. Colors. Silence. Monks alarmed. Encampment.......... 166

XXV.—THE FIRST DESERT TROUBLE, THIRST.

Waiting on the farther shore. Supplies for the journey. A celebration. Dancing. First day's travel. Second day. Third day. Delusion and disappointment. Marah. Elim............ 174

XXVI.—A NEW TROUBLE, HUNGER.

Time from Egypt to Sinai. Happy valley. A long march. The mountains in sight. Encampment by the sea. Wilderness of Sin. Provisions exhausted. Quails. Manna. The Sabbath 182

XXVII.—THE NEXT STAGE, THIRST AGAIN.

Dophkah and Alush. Wady Feiran. An oasis. Rephidim. More murmuring. The smitten rock. Water. That rock was Christ............ 190

XXVIII.—WAR.

The desert not uninhabited. Amalekites. Plunderers. Their impiety. A challenge for battle. A gallant assault. Joshua. Holding up Moses' hands. Visitors in camp. Good advice well followed............ 196

XXIX.—THE MOUNT OF GOD.

Mount Serbal. Lepsius. Circuitous course. An open plain. Three mountain heads. Sinai and Horeb. Another date. Remembering the way. Waiting for God............ 202

XXX.—GIVING THE LAW.

Moses called up into the mountain. A mediator. An election. A visible God. Preparation to receive the King. Daybreak alarm. The cloud, the smoke and the trumpet. Bounds. Gazing on the God. The law 209

XXXI.—IN THE MOUNT.

Angelic attendance. Where God was. The covenant angel. The election ratified. Singular ceremony. The blood of the covenant. "They saw God".. 216

XXXII.—FIRST GREAT REVOLT.

Moses and Joshua six days before the Lord. Moses goes up higher. The camp quiet. Rising uneasiness at Moses' absence. Sense-conception. Idolatry its origin. They want a god. Aaron's character. The demand for the jewels. The people in earnest. Seeking delays. The day comes. A heathen festival. Moses' return to camp. Not the meekest man. Vigorous measures. The broken prayer.................................. 223

XXXIII.—THE PLAN OF GOD.

The mission of the Hebrew people. Abraham. Sifting the seed. A solitary people. Discipline in Egypt. Types of things invisible. A primitive people. The same mission now performed by the Church.. 234

XXXIV.—THE GREAT KING.

What sort of government. Not a republic. Not a monarchy. A theocracy. Impossible to forget God. False worship was treason. Court etiquette. Earthly rewards and punishments. The Levitical service. The offerings and sacrifices. Spiritual meaning 239

XXXV.—THE KING'S HOUSE.

The people at work. Trades learned in Egypt. Inspired architects. The house. The attendants of the king. The cloud-chariot. Double meaning. The demand for blood. Religious ideas developed 247

XXXVI.—TAKING THE CENSUS.

The book of Numbers. Another date. A military organization. The census of each tribe. The grand army in four divisions. Order of encampment. Special arrangements for the Levites.. 255

XXXVII.—ENFORCING THE LAWS.

Two young priests. Strange fire. Unauthorized worship. No mourning for dead rebels. The priests at service to drink no wine. Profane swearing. What comes of a quarrel. Death penalty 261

XXXVIII.—BREAKING CAMP.

How long they waited at Sinai. Date of departure. Ceremony for commencing a march. Direction they moved. The home of Raguel, Jethro and Hobab. An invitation. End of the first stage.. 266

XXXIX.—MURMURINGS.

Taberah. What did they complain of? The mixed multitude. A fire from the Lord. Dainty appetites. "This manna." Foolish children. Crying for an onion. Appointment of the seventy. A flock of quails. Kibroth-hattaavah.................. 269

XL.—A FAMILY QUARREL.

PAGE

Domestic affairs and state affairs. Aaron and Miriam. The Ethiopian woman. Miriam overshadowed. Going to God with the troubles. Miriam smitten. Aaron's truculence. Moses' prayer.. 277

XLI.—A LOST OPPORTUNITY.

Twenty encampings in an eleven days' journey. Early September. Coming out of the desert. Kadesh-barnea. Spies. A good report with a bad appendage. A minority report. Exaggerations. Alarm. Revolt. Divine interposition. A threatening. Moses' prayer. Forty years more. Reaction of feeling. Failure... 283

XLII.—A SABBATH LESSON.

Gathering sticks. The offender arrested. What his offence was. Presumptuous sin. Open defiance of God's law. The man stoned. Sabbath laws.. 291

XLIII.—REBELLION.

A discontented element. Moses and his God. The old ranks and orders. Reuben the first-born. The Kohathites. Going again to God. A proposition. Fire from God. Korah and his company.. 294

XLIV.—NOT YET SATISFIED.

The persistence of wickedness. Another murmuring. Another threatening. Between the living and the dead. The rods of the tribes. The buds and the blossoms.............................. 301

XLV.—THE PLACE OF THE WANDERINGS.

A deep cleft in the earth. Valley of the Jordan. Valley of Arabah. Mount Hor. Petra. Desert of Tih. Their forty years' home. Feeling their way eastward. The ninetieth Psalm. The new nation....... 305

XLVI.—NEW ACQUAINTANCES.

A date. The old nation and the new. Murmurings. Miriam's death. A great disappointment. No punishment this time. Moses' offence. What? Moses and Aaron under a frown of God....... 311

XLVII.—DEATH OF AARON.

Route from Kadesh-barnea. Arabah again. Mount Hor. A sad announcement. The event timely. Dying grandly. Up the mountain. Mourning. A saint of God....... 315

XLVIII.—THE FIERY SERPENTS.

Ezion-geber. Turning eastward. Then northward. A terrible country. More murmurings. Serpents. The singular remedy. Why? What became of the brazen serpent....... 320

XLIX.—TWO GREAT BATTLES.

A populous country. Its disadvantages. No passage through Moab. Land of the Amorites. Sihon. A battle. A kingdom not promised. Og and Bashan. Another conquest. Effect on the Hebrews. God as good as his word....... 324

L.—A CONJURER.

Moabites among the Amorites. Balak. His plan to dispose of Moses. Supernatural means. The man he needs. Sends in vain. Falsehood met by reality....... 328

LI.—THE CURSE AND THE BLESSING.

Balaam. A money argument. Larger offers. Permission to go. An adventure. A colloquy. An angel. On the terrace. Prophetic rhapsody. A later plan more effective.................. 331

LII.—DEATH OF MOSES.

Time to go over. One act more. A valedictory and a death-song. Death like Aaron's. Moses' physical vigor. The scene. His history. Canaan melting into heaven. The wise choice.. 338

LIST OF ILLUSTRATIONS.

	PAGE
SCENE ON THE NILE	FRONTISPIECE.
STATUE OF AN EGYPTIAN KING, NEAR IPSAMBUL	23
THE PAPYRUS	28
THE FINDING OF MOSES	32
MAP OF THE JOURNEYINGS OF THE CHILDREN OF ISRAEL	37
PORTICO OF EGYPTIAN TEMPLE	45
PUTTING OFF THE SHOES	57
EGYPTIAN SANDALS	58
ORIENTAL SALUTATION	58
RAMESES II., THE PHARAOH OF MOSES. (From Lepsius.)	73
BRICK-MAKING IN EGYPT	77
THE BASTINADO	81
SCARABÆUS SACER	103
THE LOCUST	122
AMUN-RA	125
EGYPTIAN WOMEN AND THEIR JEWELS	130
HYSSOP	134
DEATH OF THE FIRST-BORN	137
EGYPTIAN SPINNING AND WEAVING	145
MAP OF THE JOURNEYINGS OF THE ISRAELITES FROM THE CROSSING OF THE RED SEA TO SINAI	147
EGYPTIAN CHARIOT	153
MAP OF MOUNT SINAI AND ITS VICINITY	203
MOUNT SINAI	207
APIS	229
THE HIGH PRIEST	244
THE TABERNACLE	248
GROUND PLAN OF THE TABERNACLE	249
THE ALTAR OF BURNT-OFFERING	252
GROUND PLAN OF ENCAMPMENT	258
ANCIENT CENSER. (From Montfaucon.)	303
MAP OF THE JOURNEYINGS OF THE CHILDREN OF ISRAEL FROM MOUNT SINAI TO JORDAN	307
THE SUMMIT OF MOUNT HOR, SEEN FROM THE SOUTH-EAST	316

ACROSS THE DESERT.

I.

THE WONDER-LAND.

THE interest of a narrative depends largely upon the conception one has of the natural scenery amid which the events narrated occurred. Certainly no life of Moses can be well presented without an account of the land of Egypt. It was in that remarkable country that he was born, and among that singular people that he was educated; and it was from that land that he led forth the people of God.

To form a mental picture of Egypt, we set before ourselves, first, a wide waste of drifting sand. This is a section of the great African Desert, terminating on the north at the Mediterranean Sea and on the east at the Red Sea.

Now, beginning at a point where this dreary country borders on the Mediterranean, let us draw a line directly southward till we reach the

Abyssinian Mountains. See! As we make our mark the limestone rock on which our sand-waste rests splits asunder, opening a deep cleft, and on each side the ledges so formed retire, carrying the sands with them and leaving a valley several miles in width. Seen from that valley, those ledges have the appearance of low mountain-ranges, and at various points lateral gorges break through them up into the desert.

. Now, beginning at the southern extremity of this valley, let us draw another line with a waving motion down through its centre. Look again! A broad and deep river follows the mark you make, carrying the waters of the far south northward to the Mediterranean. That river is the Nile, and as the barren soil begins to feel the unaccustomed touch of moisture, the valley clothes itself with green.* Soon goats and sheep are there browsing the fragrant clover. Then palm trees lift their heads and toss their feathery plumes against the cloudless sky. Then the birds come—birds of the brightest plumage and the sweetest song. And last of all comes man. This valley constitutes the land of Egypt. We will call it the Wonder-land. The Israelites called it the House of Bondage.

* Stanley.

Near the Mediterranean this valley spreads out into what is called the Delta, like an open fan, and the Nile, as if on purpose to accommodate this wider surface, divides itself into several streams. This Delta, so named from its resemblance to the Greek letter Delta [Δ], was anciently called Lower Egypt, and is the only part of the country spoken of in Mosaic history.* On the easternmost border of this Delta, skirting the easternmost branch of the Nile, was the land of Goshen, the region occupied by the Hebrew people. This province, near the river, was very fertile—there was no better land in Egypt; but out toward the desert it was mostly mere pasture-ground. Pharaoh had assigned this region to the Hebrews, and its good pasturage was a prime recommendation with them, as they were keepers of cattle. As their numbers increased, however, and they turned their attention to agriculture, they took more and more possession of the rich bottom-lands along the Nile, thus at length occupying nearly the whole province of Goshen.

No rain falls in Egypt, or nearly none, and yet about midsummer the river begins to rise. This is owing to rains near the source of one of

---

* Hawks' Egypt, page 68.

its principal branches* in the Abyssinian country. In September it overflows its banks. A little later it begins to retire again to its usual channel, leaving a rich top-dressing on all the fields. This deposit, of course, slightly elevates the banks each year, and in the process of some centuries the elevation becomes very noticeable. Meanwhile, the bed of the river is also built up by the sand and heavy deposit which come down with each flood, and so the Nile Valley is quite convex,† the whole river with its banks and bed being lifted above those portions of the country lying farther from the stream. This circumstance is taken advantage of in the irrigation of the soil, and at the time of the flood it gives the river a wide overflow.

Without its river Egypt would be a desert waste, and partly in recognition of this fact, and partly on account of the mystery attending its annual overflow, the Egyptians regarded it as a sacred stream and worshiped it as a god.

Egypt is the first country in which we find an organized government with settled political institutions. The Pharaohs who ruled over it were men of great authority, and the people under them, with the exception of the priestly caste,

---

* The Blue Nile. † Hawks, page 67.

were little better than slaves. Hence the colossal monuments they were able to rear, the ruins of which still excite the wonder of the world.

Every representation made of a reigning monarch was replete with majesty. The picture of a king was drawn ten times as large as that of an

STATUE OF AN EGYPTIAN KING NEAR IPSAMBUL.

ordinary man—the same size as a picture of one of the gods; and when a royal statue was erected, it was hewn from solid granite, and sometimes reached the height of seventy-five feet, though in a sitting posture.* Such statues in those an-

* Stanley.

cient cities must have lifted their heads above all the house-roofs, like our church towers. Even the oath in Egypt was "by the life of Pharaoh;" and when the Hebrew Jehovah sent a command to one of these majestic beings, he sent back for answer, "I am Pharaoh. Who is Jehovah?"

It was once the fashion to say that the Pharaoh who reigned in the days of Joseph was a usurper—one of a dynasty of usurpers known as Hyksos or shepherd kings. This, it was said, accounted for his kindness to the Hebrews, who were shepherds; and as shepherds were an abomination to the true Egyptian, it was held that the expulsion of these shepherd kings and the restoration of the old dynasty brought the Hebrews into sudden disfavor. Very few of our best scholars,* however, at the present day, entertain this view. Some go so far as to deny the whole story of the Hyksos. Others accept the story, but place the expulsion of those invaders far before Joseph's time.

For some reason, however, the Hebrews fell into disfavor in Egypt. The pretence was that they were becoming dangerous to the state on account of their numbers, and to prevent their increase and to keep them in subjection, the

* Hengstenberg's Egypt and Books of Moses.

reigning sovereign began to practice upon them the severest cruelties. This change in their lot occurred about five years before the birth of Moses.*

II.

OUTCAST.

PHARAOH crowned all his previous acts of oppression upon the Hebrews by making a law to destroy all their male children: "And Pharaoh charged all his people, saying, Every son that is born ye shall cast into the river." Ex. i. 22. But there were some things which even a Pharaoh could not do, and the command to destroy those children was never carefully obeyed. In some cases the parents would hide their children; in other cases the persons appointed to execute the edict would make excuses and evade the law.

Among the children born at this eventful period was Moses. His father's name was Amram, his mother's Jochebed, and they were of the tribe of Levi. Whether they were persons of wealth or not, whether they enjoyed any social distinction or not, or whether in any way

* Hawks' Egypt, pages 174, 175.

their lot was distinguished from that of the rest of those suffering people, we are not informed. On a more important point, however, we fortunately have some light. "By faith Moses, when he was born, was hid of his parents three months, because they saw that he was a proper child; and they were not afraid of the king's commandment." Heb. xi. 23. They were people who had faith—in other words, they were religious people; and, as such, they ventured upon the extraordinary measure of setting themselves to disobey a law of Pharaoh. They trusted in God and undertook to save their child.

When he is called a "proper child," we do not at once take the meaning. The expression has reference to his great natural beauty. So Stephen says of him that he was "exceeding fair" (Acts vii. 20), or, as it might have been rendered, divinely beautiful. And Josephus perpetuates a tradition to the effect that persons who met him as he was carried along the street were sometimes so fascinated by his loveliness as to pause and turn back to gaze after him.

Now it was well understood among the Hebrew people that Egypt was not to be their permanent home. In due time, as they believed, their nation would return to the land promised to their fathers, and they knew that the four hundred years of waiting, reckoning from the time of Abraham, was nearly at an end. Naturally, therefore, they expected a deliverer to arise among them; and when this extraordinary child appeared in the house of Amram, the parents, at least, would be quite ready to inquire whether this should not be he who should bring them out of the house of bondage.

For three months, therefore, they periled their own lives by keeping the child hid. Then, perhaps threatened with a search, and knowing that concealment was no longer possible, they prepared, in the letter at least, to obey the king's commandment by casting him into the river. The law did not prescribe the mode in which the act should be performed; why could they not put the child upon something which, at least for a time, would keep him afloat? So his mother "took for him an ark of bulrushes and put the child therein, and laid him in the flags by the river's brink. And his sister stood afar off, to wit what would become of him."

The bulrushes here spoken of were a species of the celebrated Egyptian papyrus or paper-plant.* It is not strictly a rush, as our transla-

* Rawlinson's Herodotus, ii. 129.

tion would imply, but of the family of sedges. It grew in marshy ground and along the shallow margin of the Nile, running up at times to the height of ten or twelve feet. Usually, how-

PAPYRUS.

ever, its height was not more than six feet. The stem of the plant is of the usual reed form, and of a light green color, terminating in a crown of filaments something like broom-corn.

In a country producing no forests and having but few sorts of trees suitable for timber, it requires some ingenuity to construct a boat. This difficulty the Egyptians overcame in part by making boats of papyrus. They would obtain, perhaps from the acacia tree, a suitable stick for a keel, and then would plait these stalks of papyrus upon it, something after the fashion of basket-work, and so form quite a little vessel. The interstices they filled with pitch or slime, which was probably asphaltum brought from the vicinity of the Dead Sea.

When Moses' mother, therefore, wished to make a little boat in which to float her child, she also had recourse to bulrushes, pitch and slime. She called her boat an ark. It was an imitation of the sailing craft which she had often seen on the river Nile. When it was finished and well dried, it made a beautiful cradle for her babe, and the flags amid which she laid it prevented it from immediately floating away.

Taken from a mere human view, her experiment was a very hazardous one. The Nile was the home of the crocodile, that hateful beast worshiped in Egypt as one of the gods. A grand sacrifice would this child be to such a deity—a right tempting morsel for those cavernous jaws. It required some decision of character to put such a plan in execution, but in desperate circumstances people are sometimes roused to do desperate things.

III.

PHARAOH'S DAUGHTER.

IT was customary to bathe in the Nile. This was partly for health and comfort, but more for a religious service. The stream was sacred, and its waters were supposed to wash out the stains which sin makes upon the soul. We shall find, by and by, that it was customary to take a morning hour for these ablutions. Ex. vii. 15. If such were the only hour for this ceremonial, it would help us to an interesting particular of our story. The infant Moses was found by Pharaoh's daughter when she went down to the stream to bathe. If this were morning, we can guess at what hour the little ark was laid among the flags. It must have been done as early as the first daybreak, and before people were stirring.

They had not slept much in that Hebrew home the last night. Hasty preparations were made to finish the ark, to dry the bitumen and to line it softly for the reception of its treasure. Then, before the stars had disappeared, they had put the child asleep, laid it in its new cradle and hastily gone out with it to the river bank. They carried it down the slope and waded out with it a little way among the flags; then they softly set it down, and it floated on the water. Miriam, the child's sister, now perhaps ten years old, was left to see what became of it.

Pharaoh's palace was hard by. Whether it was his country palace, where he was merely passing the season, or whether this Hebrew family dwelt in the suburbs of the capital city, we cannot tell, but it was by no mere chance, we may well suppose, that they placed the little ark where some one would come to bathe.

Directly, therefore, down came Pharaoh's daughter, and Miriam, Moses' sister, watched her at every step. She had some maidens with her to wait upon her, and together they descended to the water's edge. What was that just yonder among the sedge—that little boat so nicely woven and so carefully covered? Woman's curiosity was roused, and the nimble maidens plunged in after it and soon brought it ashore. They took off the cover, and what a surprise! A babe! and such a beautiful babe! Child of the Nile god this must be, and she calls his name Moses—*drawn out* of the water. The story is

THE FINDING OF MOSES.

briefly told in Scripture, but not without a touch of pathos: "She sent her maid to fetch it, and when she had opened it she saw the child; and the babe wept."

Almost any heart would have been touched by

such a sight. To the heart of a gentle woman it presented an appeal that was irresistible. She knew that this must be one of the Hebrew children, and she knew the king's commandment, but could she resist the eloquence of that inarticulate voice, that beautiful face, those uplifted hands? What advantage was it to her to be Pharaoh's daughter unless she could claim some privilege under Pharaoh's law? So presuming on her position, she ventured to do what no other person perhaps in the empire would have dared. She took the child and resolved to save it; and to make the act effective, she adopted it on the spot and made it her own.

But what could she do with it? To bring it directly to the palace might not be the best policy. Besides, the care of it while so young would interrupt her pleasures. If she could find a nurse for it! Perhaps it was while this thought was in her mind that Miriam came up. "Would the king's daughter like to engage a nurse to take care of the child she had found?" This query settled the case. The little maiden was sent to find a nurse, and of course brought the child's own mother. "And Pharaoh's daughter said, Take this child and nurse it for me, and I will give thee thy wages."

c

One would judge from the narrative that the king's daughter had no idea that she was committing the child to its mother, and if such were the case, it speaks something for Jochebed. To have so perfectly acted her part in this little drama as to awaken no suspicion indicates a rare faculty of self-control. To take that babe in her arms again, to be ordered by the king's daughter to act as its nurse and to be actually paid for so doing was so sudden a change of circumstances as would have overpowered any ordinary mind, and so have baulked the whole plan. But when she had got home again with her treasure, she could indulge her feeling. "I will give thee thy wages," one hears her say. "Is it not wages enough to take in my arms once more my beautiful boy?" Then how she would press the child to her heart! And when Amram came home that day from his task-work and was told what had happened, one imagines them breaking out with one voice in a song of praise to their fathers' God.

Things were now well arranged for the child. For the present, at least, he was safe. The officers might come and search the house if they chose. This child was the ward of Pharaoh's daughter. Who dare lay hands on him? As soon as he should be grown up, however, he would have to go out from his Hebrew home and try the temptations of the royal palace. Within ten or twelve years everything must be done that was ever to be done to instruct and confirm this young mind in the religion of his people. And that good mother, in whom we have already caught a glimpse of some rare qualities, was the appointed instrument for the work. How she prayed with him, how she repeated to him again and again the traditions of her people, how she told him of Abraham and Noah and Joseph, one can well imagine. By such stories she would make him see what an honor it was to be a Hebrew, and how her people, though oppressed, were still the dear people of the Lord. Those few years must have been well improved. When he left home, two principles had been thoroughly rooted in his soul. One was that he was never to forsake his people; the other was that he was never to forsake his mother's God.

IV.

IN THE HOUSE OF PHARAOH.

"THE child grew, and she brought him unto Pharaoh's daughter, and he became her son." Ex: ii. 10. It was a great change—up from that humble Hebrew home to the palace of the king; and Moses was to be tested whether, like many another since his day, the sudden elevation would not prove his ruin. The case was much like that of Daniel afterward at the court of Babylon, and perhaps Daniel learned from this example that fidelity to God which he so beautifully exhibited.

How far Moses would be indulged in the peculiarities of his religion, or what firmness it may have required to sustain his character as a true Hebrew worshiper, we can only surmise. One sentence contains nearly all the information the Bible furnishes of his entire life of nearly thirty years at the Egyptian court: "And Moses was learned in all the wisdom of the Egyptians, and was mighty in words and in deeds." Acts vii. 22.

The learning of the Egyptians was largely in the hands of the priestly caste, and perhaps it was at first intended to educate Moses for sacred

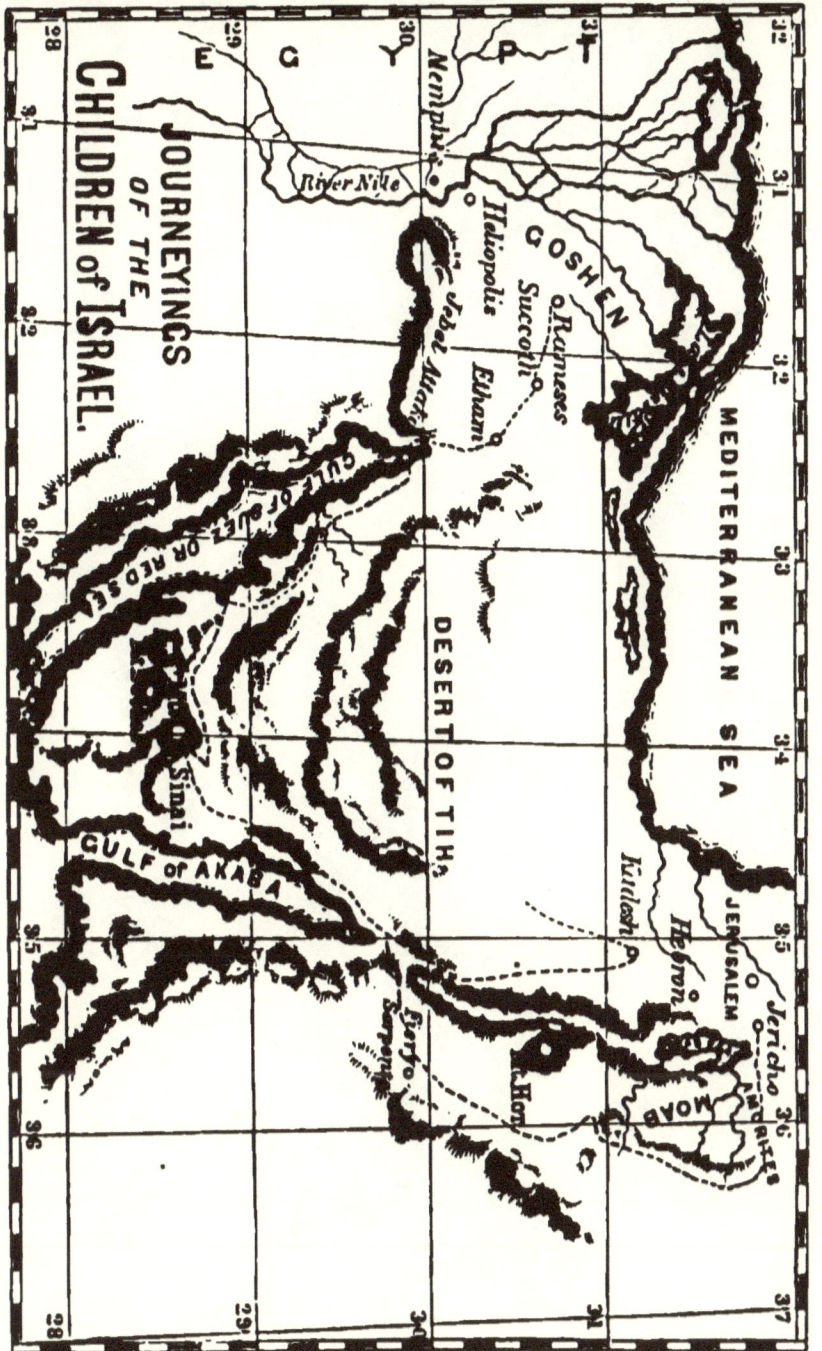

orders.* If he could be made a priest, it would have some effect to bring his people over to the national religion. But if this were the plan, it was given up. Moses' convictions were already too fixed to change. Those magnificent temples whose remains still astonish the world were not to be the scenes of his activity. A new experiment was perhaps made with him in the line of statesmanship and military affairs. He was put to the study of government and the study of war; and if so, this would be exactly what he would need when he should take charge of the Hebrew people. If he was learned in all the wisdom of the Egyptians, he was one of the best scholars of his times, for in learning the Egyptians then led the world. So we see that God, in choosing an instrument for his great work, selected an educated man.

Some will doubt whether this were necessary. God can endow his servants with all needful qualifications without the use of schools, and Moses was continually receiving instruction directly from a divine source. What was the necessity of educating him? The answer to this question is, that God's plan is not to endow men supernaturally with qualifications which

* Stanley's Jewish Church, page 117.

they can just as well obtain in some other way. What Moses needed to know in order to organize and administer a new government he could learn at the court of Pharaoh. What he needed to learn in order to establish a new religious economy he was obliged to receive by inspiration of God. These two things were indeed greatly intermingled in the office which he filled, but the general principle prevailed that Moses was directly taught of God only in such things as he could not learn from any accessible human source.

The "mighty words" of Moses strike one as constituting an important variation from the popular idea of his abilities. He himself says that he is a man of "slow speech," and the common idea of him is that, in oratorical power at least, he was somewhat deficient. But even Paul, whose voice woke the world, speaks of himself disparagingly (1 Cor. ii. 4) in this particular, and it may be that both these men underrated their own gifts. There were certainly some occasions on which Moses was eloquent, and his written words, at any rate, are mighty through God. He even indulged himself in poetry when occasion offered, and so long as men appreciate religious fervor and lofty expression the world will not forget his psalm (the ninetieth) and his song at the sea.

The Jews have a tradition that he once led a military expedition into the Ethiopian country. It is not unlikely that such may have been the case. Those Pharaohs were quick to recognize competent men, and such a mind as that of Moses would not be long unemployed at the Egyptian court. So he was put in practice, most likely, in those very things which he would soon most need to understand. Thus those years in the house of Pharaoh were years of most important preparation for the work to which he was predestined.

When God intends to accomplish anything, he is never at a loss for instruments. When he wanted a deliverer for Israel, he chose that outcast child. When he wanted the child rescued and protected, he sent the king's daughter to do it. To give him an education in the Hebrew religion he returned him to his mother and kept him under her influence through all his tender years. To train him to govern men and manage public affairs he opened for him the Egyptian schools and put him in practice under the hand of the Egyptian king.

V.

IN THE HOUSE OF BONDAGE. [B. C. 1531.]

THE plan of exterminating the Hebrew race was given over. It could not be effected. Besides, they could be put to better uses. The king wanted to fortify that Goshen country where they dwelt against any future incursions from the nomadic races east and north of him. Who so good to build his fortifications as these same Hebrews? He would have two walled cities —treasure cities he called them, but they were more of the nature of immense forts.* So he appointed taskmasters over the Hebrews, who should set them in labor-gangs to make brick and build those great walls.

The work, once organized, went briskly on. So profitable a service, once discovered, was not likely to be discontinued, and a period of many years is doubtless covered by the statement that "they made their lives bitter with hard bondage, in mortar, and in brick, and in all manner of service of the field. And they built Pithom and Raamses." Ex. i. 11, 14.

These hardships were nothing diminished, but

---

* Hawks' Egypt, page 178.

PORTICO OF EGYPTIAN TEMPLE.

rather increased while Moses was in the house of Pharaoh. The people were never, indeed, precisely made slaves, for they dwelt in houses of their own and were owners of flocks and cattle, but this terrible labor-tax ground them down to the earth. Moses heard of it in the palace: "And when he was grown he went out unto his brethren and looked upon their burdens."

He was now about forty years old (Acts vii. 23); and after witnessing the sufferings of his people till he could endure the sight no longer, he resolved to turn his back upon the Egyptian court and undertake the defence of the Hebrews. He must have held a very high position at court. The son of Pharaoh's daughter was not a man that need go out as an adventurer, but he never could forget that he was a Hebrew; and when he saw the indignities and atrocities practiced upon those poor men, he pushed aside the inviting prospects before him and went down to identify himself with their cause.

He was not so cautious in this as he might have been—he was too ready to take it for granted that the people would rally at his call; and he soon learned that, though his impulses might be generous, he would have done better to wait for divine direction. In attempting to defend his people he killed an Egyptian. In a subsequent attempt to settle a quarrel between two Hebrews his crime was flouted against him. And within perhaps three days from the time he left court he found that the people were not ready for deliverance.

His next thought was for his own safety. He had killed a government officer in defence of the man on whom the officer was inflicting the usual punishment of the times. The act was well known among the Hebrews, at least, and they were none too good to appear against him before Pharaoh. He saw that he would do well to get out of harm's way.

Yet he was not sorry, perhaps, that he had left the court. That was no congenial place for such a man as he. The people might reject him, and God might choose some other man to lead them out to liberty. But they were God's people, nevertheless, and with them he desired to cast in his lot. He had entered upon this business under a solemn religious conviction. He had turned his back upon the pleasures of the house of Pharaoh because they were "pleasures of sin." Heb. xi. 24. He had chosen to suffer affliction rather than be separated from the Lord's people; and if his plans had miscarried, he regretted it more on their account than his own. If God chose to raise up another deliverer and set him aside, he had no complaints to make. He was quite ready to retire.

VI.

IN A STRANGE LAND.

DIRECTLY to the south-east of the province of Goshen is a region of country known in modern geography as the peninsula of Sinai. It is a triangularly-shaped district, with its apex toward the south, and seems driven in like a wedge between the two arms of the Red Sea. In the Scriptures it is sometimes called the Desert, sometimes the land of Midian, and sometimes Arabia, though Arabia is a term usually embracing considerable additional territory.

This peninsula has a peculiar formation. Though a desert, it is not so much a desert of sand as one of rock, and some subterranean force seems to have lifted the central mass, thrusting up numerous granite pinnacles against the sky and breaking great rifts from the centre down toward either shore. These rifts, which are called wadys, form natural watercourses, and in winter they are swept by an occasional flood, but for the most part they are perfectly dry, affording the only practicable communication with the interior.

Here and there in this desolate region a little moisture is found, and wherever there is moisture there is vegetation. But with these exceptions the country is utterly waste, and the only inhabitants are some wandering tribes that feed their flocks along the scanty pasture-grounds. The absence of life renders it a very silent country, and from one end of the land to the other scarce the hum of an insect vibrates on the ear.* In Moses' day it was probably somewhat more productive than now, and consequently more populous; but then, as now, it stood an awful solitude known as "the great and terrible desert."

When Moses saw that he could no longer remain safely in Egypt, it was to this land that he took his flight. Passing round the Gulf of Suez, he followed the eastern shore till he struck one of those great wadys which opened into the interior. This he followed till he reached the central heights known as the Horeb country, when he passed down the watershed toward the Gulf

---

* Stanley's Sinai and Palestine, page 14.

of Akabah. He had been journeying perhaps nearly a week, and was now well out of the reach of pursuit, when he sat down one day to rest by a well. Near him dwelt a chieftain of some Midianitish tribe, who, according to patriarchal custom, was not only a prince, but a priest. His rank was not very high, however, for we find his own daughters, seven in number, keeping his sheep, and it shows how little authority he wielded, that while Moses sat at the well those daughters came to water their flocks, and when they had filled the watering-troughs some shepherds dashed in upon them to drive them away. It could not have been a very powerful chieftain against whom such an offence would have been ventured.

Here comes out one of the marked features of Moses' character. He was a man who had the warmest sympathy with the oppressed, and the instant he sees these maidens likely to be driven off he springs forward in their defence. Moses is traditionally "the meekest man," but when roused he was tremendously energetic. How he was roused on this occasion one may judge by what he did. Those rough men that were driving away the chieftain's daughters were not the sort of people to be easily frightened; and if Moses beat them off, it must have been by some pretty vigorous handling of them. One sees him hurling one to the ground, grasping another by the throat, menacing a third with his disengaged hand, and making such an onset as made them glad enough to give way.

It was a right gallant affair, and was well rewarded. Jacob, in similar circumstances, met Rachel at Padan-aram, and was fain to serve her father seven years that he might make her his wife. Moses paid his dowry in this fight, his chivalry winning for him his prize in one short hour.

The name of the chieftain whose daughters Moses thus defended was Raguel or Reuel. His daughters reported the good behavior of "the Egyptian," as they called Moses, and he was invited to the hospitalities of the family. "And Moses was content to dwell with the man, and he gave him Zipporah his daughter." Ex. ii. 21.

A sudden change was it for Moses—from the wheatfields of Egypt to the rocky desert of Horeb, from the busy city to this awful solitude, from the palace of Pharaoh to the tent of Raguel, from the great burden of empire to the care of a flock of sheep—a change so great that, coming suddenly, few men could have borne it. But Moses was perhaps weary of public life, and the quiet of that distant region might have been welcome to his soul.

God had a plan in sending him there. Such a man as he needed not only the discipline of public life, but equally the discipline of solitude. There is also reason to believe that Raguel was a worshiper of the true God (Ex. xviii. 9–12), and it may be that in his seclusion he had retained the purity of his faith better than the Israelites had done in Egypt. There might have been something for Moses to learn from Raguel concerning God. Besides, Moses was to lead the great caravan of the Israelites through that country, and it was well to explore it beforehand. Forty years' residence there must have acquainted him with every pass and peak and well and spring and spot of verdure in all that land. Moreover, as it was near Palestine, and Moses knew that the latter was promised to his people, it is not unreasonable to suppose that he made now and then an excursion thither, the better to understand what treasures God had in waiting for them. But above all was this solitary land a good place in which to hold communion with God, and to receive from him those revelations which were necessary in writing the early history of the world.

For forty years, therefore, Moses dwelt in the desert. Some would have called it waste time, but perhaps it was worth as much to him, with reference to his future work, as the corresponding period passed at the house of Pharaoh.

VII.

A VOICE. [B. C. 1491.]

THE forty years which Moses spent in the desert were marked by some important changes. One of these was the death of Pharaoh and the accession of a new monarch to the throne of Egypt bearing the same name. Another was a change in Moses himself, who has gone on from forty years of age to eighty, and who, though in full vigor, is yet an old man. Still another of these changes appears in the name of Moses' employer, and hereby hangs a question.

Forty years ago Moses entered the service of Raguel, marrying his daughter; now his master's name is Jethro. Ex. iii. 1. Our English translation of the Scriptures adopts the supposition that Jethro and Raguel were the same person, and all through the third chapter of Exodus

Jethro is set forth as Moses' father-in-law. But the Hebrew word [chothen] translated father-in-law would be just as correctly rendered brother-in-law.* It is a general term applicable to any person nearly related by marriage. And though it is possible that Jethro is Raguel under a new name, it is more probable that Raguel is dead, and that Jethro is his eldest son.

When Moses arrived in Midian, Raguel was old enough to be the father of seven daughters, all of whom were of sufficient age to be keepers of his flocks. He must, therefore, have been married something like thirty years. But men in that age seldom married till they were about forty years old, as we see in the case of Isaac, Jacob and Moses, so that Raguel must have been about seventy years old when Moses made his acquaintance. Add to this the forty years spent in his service, and he would now be one hundred and ten years old. But outside the Hebrew family human life very rarely extended to that term. Herodotus, in his day, reckons three generations to a century, making average life about the same then as now;† and Moses himself, in the ninetieth psalm, says, "The days of our years are threescore

---

* Bush, Calmet, etc., in Loc.
† Rawlinson's Herodotus, ii. 189.

years and ten." While, therefore, it is possible that Raguel was still living, and that he comes before us under the new name of Jethro, it is more probable that he was dead, and that Jethro had succeeded to his estate. On that supposition, Moses, as connected with the family by marriage, and as a long-tried and faithful helper, would very naturally continue in their employment.

Dean Stanley supposes that Jethro lived beyond the interior solitudes of Horeb, not far from the Gulf of Akabah. Probably he takes this supposition from the words, "the back side of the desert" (Ex. iii. 1), signifying the side beyond the mountain, as related to Egypt. But wherever Jethro lived, Moses loved those great solitudes near Horeb itself; and as there were several springs in that region and some good spots of pasture, he often led his flocks there to pass his days alone with God.

One of the chief vegetable productions of this region is the acacia tree, known in later times as shittim wood. It is, perhaps, an exaggeration to speak of this production as a tree, for it is more of the nature of a bush, but it is quite a tree for that country, sometimes growing to the height of twenty feet. The species growing in Egypt, which the author saw in his recent visit to that country, considerably resembles our common locust tree, and that in the desert is much the same, only smaller and more bushy. Bishop Keble calls it the "towering thorn," and Dean Stanley describes it as an object of great beauty, "shooting out its gay foliage and blue blossoms over the desert." * One species furnishes the gum arabic of commerce, and its wood afforded the only available timber for building the tabernacle. The Hebrews call it seneh, the thorn, and from this term the word Sinai is supposed to be derived.†

One day, while Moses was leading his flock in that region, he saw one of these trees apparently on fire. Naturally a little startled at first, he would, on reflection, soon conclude, perhaps, that the fire had been kindled by some wandering band of Amalekites, and then he would begin to be anxious for the safety of his flock. But on looking closely he saw that this fire did not burn the tree. There it stood, the flames leaping among the branches, and perhaps roaring in his hearing, but not a leaf was withered nor a twig consumed.

This thoroughly aroused him, and he said, "I

---

* Sinai and Palestine, 69.   † Bush.

will turn aside and see this great sight." But no sooner did he approach the tree than a Voice called to him out of the midst of the fire, saying, "Draw not nigh hither, but put off thy shoe from off thy foot, for the place where thou standest is holy ground."

Moses has heard how God used to visit his people and talk with them, but that was in old times. The last authentic account of such an occurrence was on the occasion of Jacob's going down into Egypt, which was at least two hundred and fifteen years ago—some say four hundred years ago. Now, the conviction is rapidly being forced upon him that God is speaking again. If Moses had any doubt on that subject, it is soon put at rest, for the Voice says, "I am the God of thy father, the God of Abraham, and the God of Isaac, and the God of Jacob."

At the opening of this story in the book of Exodus (Ex iii., 2) the person who appeared in the burning bush is called an angel. Here he is called God. This mode of speech is many times repeated in the Old Testament, and this angel is supposed to be the second person of the Trinity, called an angel because he acts as messenger between heaven and earth. The Son of God, in these cases, anticipated his coming in human flesh, and presented himself by voice and form, as if the advent had occurred already.

The command to Moses to put off his shoe was quite characteristic of the place and time.

PUTTING OFF THE SHOES.

Western nations express their reverence by uncovering the head. Of this their style of head-dress readily admits, while to remove the dress from the feet would often cause great trouble and consume no little time. Oriental nations, on the contrary, express their reverence by uncovering the feet—a thing very easy where sandals

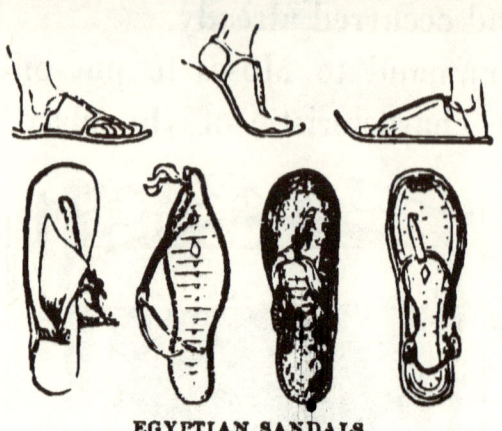

EGYPTIAN SANDALS.

are worn; whereas, to remove the turban, in some of its styles at least, and put it on again, would be a work of no small difficulty. When

ORIENTAL SALUTATION.

Moses, therefore, heard the command, he instantly put himself in a posture of reverence, and waited to hear what God would say: "And Moses hid his face, for he was afraid to look on God."

VIII.

RELUCTANCE.

WHEN Moses had thus made himself ready to hear, God spake again. He said that he had not been an inattentive observer of the sufferings of his people or of the cruelty of their oppressors. He affectionately alluded to them as the people whom he had chosen, and said that he intended to fulfill on their behalf the promises which he had made to their fathers. He told Moses of the country, great compared with Goshen, and flowing with milk and honey, which he was keeping for them, and added, "I am come down to deliver them."

Moses knew what that meant. God does not change his place indeed, but when he says that he is coming down for any purpose, men may look for thorough work. This was his language when he confounded their speech at Babel. This had been his language on the occasion of the destruction of Sodom. When God comes down, let wicked men beware.

But if this communication thus far filled Moses with joy, the remainder of the message thoroughly awakened his alarm. "Come now, therefore," said the Voice; "I will send thee unto Pharaoh."

"Send me to Pharaoh," said his heart, "and on such an errand! Why not kill me outright?" But it was not merely a fear for his personal safety; many circumstances combined to make the task an unwelcome one. Moses had dwelt in the desert till he loved it. How quietly had the years gone by! Surrounded by his family, dwelling with a tribe that worshiped the true God, and following such peaceful employments, he had hoped there to end his days. What a task was that to which he was now summoned, and that just at the period of life when men love repose! Those Hebrews! He had once tried his hand on them, and they had resented the interference. Pharaoh! It was a new man indeed of that name, but a Pharaoh nevertheless, and one who would brook neither opposition nor control.

"Who am I," cries out the weak man—"who am I that I should go unto Pharaoh?"

And the Voice answers, "I will be with thee."

Moses' next question is, "What is thy name?"

He says that the people will ask this question of him, and he wants to be able to answer them.

And God says, "Tell them I AM hath sent you: I AM THAT I AM."

Along with these communications occur several cheering utterances. God says that Moses and the Hebrews will yet one day come up and worship at that very mountain. He tells him that in going to Pharaoh he need not at first ask him squarely to set the people free. He may open negotiations with the simple request for a little respite from work to give them opportunity for a religious festival. He warns him, indeed, that Pharaoh will deny the request, but he says that such a punishment will be visited upon him that in the end he will be only too glad to send them away. And he adds that when they go they shall carry with them great spoil of silver and gold. As for the difficulty which Moses anticipates with the Hebrews themselves, God promises him a miracle-working power which shall perfectly carry their faith.

This might well have seemed sufficient, for all Moses' objections were answered. But what began in honest self-distrust degenerated into something very much like obstinacy.

"I am a man of slow speech and slow tongue,"

says Moses, as if that had anything to do with the case.

And God answered, with something like a reproof, "Who hath made man's mouth? Have not I, saith the Lord? I will be with thy mouth."

But just as little willing to go as ever, Moses answers, "O Lord, send by whom thou wilt send, only do not send me."

Then God's anger was kindled against him, and he peremptorily bade him be off to his work. Only he added that if he wanted any one to do his talking for him, Aaron, his brother, was a talking man and he might take him into service.

It was a dangerous contest into which Moses thus ventured, and we can only wonder that he should have had the hardihood to risk it. We must remember, however, that Moses knew the people whom he was sent to deliver, and had once had a most unfortunate experience with them. We must remember also that he knew the haughtiness and pride of those Pharaohs, and that he was now in the desert a fugitive from their wrath. Besides, we must again call to mind that he was now an old man, averse to new undertakings, and for forty years entirely out of service in public affairs. It was a trial to him to be sent out on such a mission, and God saw it and was patient with him. And in the end perhaps he was none the less a faithful and successful man that he had too great a misgiving at the beginning.

Aaron does not seem to have been afflicted with any such diffidence. He was a much less thoughtful man than Moses and much less to be depended on, and yet when he was ordered out to this great work he went without hesitation.

IX.

DOWN FROM THE DESERT.

WHEN Moses saw that he could not escape the solemn commission with which he was charged, he immediately set himself about the preparation to enter upon his work. First he went to Jethro and obtained an honorable release from his service; then he took "his wife and his sons and set them upon an ass," and started on his journey into Egypt.

Dean Stanley calls these his "infant sons,"[*] probably because the narrative seems to imply that they both rode on one beast at the same

[*] Jewish Church, page 128.

time with their mother. But this is only a seeming, and it is not very probable that Zipporah, who was of marriageable age forty years ago, is now the mother of two new-born children. The birth of one of them, at least, is mentioned at an early date in this history (Ex. ii. 22), and by this time they must have been grown to man's estate.

These two sons do not figure very largely in those stirring times which soon come. Their names—Gershom, a stranger, and Eliezer, God my help—commemorate their father's exile, but like the names of many another great man's sons, they sink into obscurity. Moses does not seem in any way to have put them forward or sought important positions for them. They were probably plain, humble men, unsuited to the duties of public life.

So Moses started on his journey "with the rod of God in his hand." Men in that part of the world quite commonly carry a rod in their hands. In some cases it seems intended as a kind of sceptre, indicating the rank of a chieftain. In other cases it serves as a staff, though it is much longer than an ordinary staff, usually measuring six or seven feet. In still other cases it is apparently designed as a weapon of defence, or is used to guide a flock of sheep or goats. Moses' rod was probably of this sort. God constituted it the instrument by which he was to perform his miracles.

Moses was not coming back as rich as Jacob was when he returned from Padan-aram. He had no flocks and herds with him—nothing but the one beast on which they rode by turns. He had no great household—only his wife and those two sons. He had no wealth or treasure—only that rod in his hand.

Soon after starting the party met with a great misadventure. It is said to have occurred at an inn. But we are not to imagine that there was anything in that country that we should call an inn. It is not likely that even the modern Oriental caravanserai existed there. The inn was a mere halting-place, perhaps under a palm tree, probably at a spring or a well, where it was customary to pause during the heat of the day.

"And it came to pass that the Lord met him and sought to kill him." Ex. iv. 24. Met whom? At first sight one says Moses. As one reads on he is more likely to say Gershom, the first-born. God has just been saying to Moses that if Pharaoh does not obey his voice his first-born shall be destroyed. Immediately after, Moses is put in alarm for his own first-born. God is seeking to slay him, says the record. The meaning is that the son is likely to die, and that in the disease that has suddenly come upon him they see the special interposition of the divine Hand. It is an unpromising beginning for their journey. What does it mean?

Zipporah seems to understand the case even better than her husband; at least she is first to apply the remedy. Among those Hebrews was one custom to which God attached peculiar sacredness. It was originally enjoined upon Abraham, and had now prevailed for more than four hundred years. It was the sign of the covenant between the Hebrews and God, and the law was that any person among them who had not received that token should be "cut off from his people." Gen. xvii. 14. This sign was circumcision, and it appears that Moses, dwelling apart from his people, had neglected to circumcise his son.

Now he was going down to deliver God's people with this uncircumcised son in his family—going to enter upon God's great work for the nation with this neglected duty in his own household. This was why God met him in the way. Zipporah, fully understanding the case, roused herself to meet it with a strong hand. She waited for no authorized priest. She did not even wait for Moses. The emergency was right upon her, and she circumcised the neglected son with her own hand.

Some have supposed that Moses had neglected this duty to please his wife, but the story does not well bear that meaning. She was of the Midianites, and they, as well as the Hebrews, practiced circumcision. The promptness which she displays on this occasion rather hints how many times she may have urged her husband to take up this neglected duty, and how at last she feels that an emergency has come when she must take the work in her own hands. "A bloody husband art thou to me," she said, "because of the circumcision." Ex. iv. 26. Her expedient was successful, and Gershom seems immediately to have been restored.

It was on many accounts undesirable that Moses should take his family down with him into Egypt at all. After this misadventure he seems to have gone back and put them in charge of Jethro. Then he began his journey again. Meanwhile, God had appeared to Aaron in Egypt and ordered him to meet his brother in the desert, and Moses had just reached the solitary interior when the meeting occurred. "And he went out and met him in the mount of God and kissed him." Ex. iv. 27. This is a very brief account of such a meeting as that must have been. These men were brothers— brothers who had not met before for forty years, brothers to both of whom God had just been speaking, and brothers who had been charged with a most important commission.

For Moses it was a meeting just in time. Oppressed with the magnitude of the undertaking before him, distressed at the recent mark of divine displeasure in his family, beginning a most venturesome journey alone, he needed a brother now. And Aaron was just the light-hearted, sympathetic, loquacious man to lighten his mind of its burden.

So there they go. Do you see them?—those two gray-bearded old men coming in on foot from the desert, one of them with a rod in his hand? "Whither are you traveling, old men?"

"Down into Egypt."

"And on what errand, pray?"

"To deliver the poor Hebrews there."

"And will Pharaoh let them go?"

"Not by a mighty hand. We shall have to compel him."

So one might have talked with these adventurers; and when he heard their answers he might have smiled and said, "The old men's wits are out." They went on, however, and soon were among their people, ready for their work.

X.

BEGINNING AGAIN.

FORTY years ago Moses undertook the liberation of his people, and failed in it. Now, however, affairs have changed. Then he went among them without any command of God; now he is acting under orders and can show his credentials. Then he was young; now he is old, and among that people old age commands great respect. Then he was generous, it is true, and actuated by a high religious impulse, but was somesomewhat rash; now he observes due caution and moves more wisely. Then he was alone and was comparatively a stranger; now he has Aaron with him, whom the people know and trust. Then he had no consultation with the chiefs of the tribes; now he calls together the elders of Israel; and the people themselves, after fifty years more of suffering, are, perhaps, better prepared to welcome a deliverer.

The Hebrews, though greatly crushed and broken, have from the first kept up a sort of national organization with recognized officers. The patriarchal theory still held good among them, making the father of a family priest in his house, and his eldest son both priest and prince after him. And as the eldest son of the eldest son became chief of a clan, every tribe and each branch of a tribe had an acknowledged leader and representative. So when the people wished to act together, they were in a condition to do so promptly. These heads of tribes and clans were called "elders;" and when Moses and Aaron were directed to speak to the whole congregation (Ex. xii. 3), they obeyed by calling together these representative men. Ex. xii. 21.

One of the important directions, therefore, in beginning this work, was, "Go and gather the elders of Israel." The meaning was, consult with these representative men; secure the influence of these tribal chieftains. Aaron himself, indeed, was one of these chieftains in the tribe of Levi, and on that account would command respect.

So Moses and Aaron "gathered together all the elders of the children of Israel; and Aaron spake all the words which the Lord had spoken unto Moses, and he, (*Moses,*) did the signs in the sight of the people." Ex. iv. 30. Aaron made the address because he was the appointed speaker, and Moses performed the miracles to show that God was with them.

The first of these miracles was the changing of Moses' rod into a serpent, and then changing it to a rod again. The second was making one of Moses' hands leprous, and then restoring it. The third was the changing of Nile water to blood by pouring it upon the ground. These were signs adapted to the notions of the people; and however they may strike our minds, the effect on those who witnessed them was to carry their entire conviction. The entire chieftaincy of the nation stood by and saw what was done. And when they carried back the report to their tribes, "The people believed: and when they heard that the Lord had visited the children of Israel, and that he had looked upon their afflictions, then they bowed their heads and worshiped." Ex. iv. 31.

So far, well. Moses is not rejected this time. The people welcome him as a deliverer. There is no division, or if there is it does not show itself. There is no factious minority, or if there is it is overawed. There is no jealousy of Moses' power, or if there is it does not make itself known. All the chiefs, without exception, give their voice for the movement, and as the tidings spread the nation rejoice. Best of all there is a deep religious feeling among them. They believe, they worship, they trust in God.

Now for an interview with Pharaoh; and if that succeed equally well, within ten days the people will march out to liberty and the promised land.

XI.

HOW IT STRIKES THE KING.

PHARAOH is not omniscient, and this movement among his Hebrew bondmen has not yet come to his knowledge. He has heard of Moses, perhaps has seen him, but that was forty years ago. He remembers the reputation he had at court; he remembers the mad enterprise on which he went out on behalf of his oppressed people; he knows how it terminated, and how Moses disappeared and has not since been heard of. At any rate, he has no expectation of ever seeing him again; least of all does he apprehend any harm from him.

One day, however, as he is giving audience to the people, it is announced that a delegation of the Hebrews is in waiting. "Usher them in," says the king; and as the doors are thrown open, two gray-bearded men advance at the head of a large company of their fellow-chieftains, and their names are announced: "Moses and Aaron."

The king's curiosity would at once be excited

RAMESES II., THE PHARAOH OF MOSES. (*From Lepsius.*)

to know whence came this long-absent man, and on what errand such an outlaw dared appear again at court. But he waited to hear what was wanted, and the business was immediately opened. Which of the two brothers was the speaker on this occasion we are not informed. Most likely it was Moses; for though Aaron was the more eloquent, Moses was better acquainted with the conventionalities of the palace. He says that he has come to ask the king to allow him to take the people out into the wilderness for a religious festival. He does not ask it of his own motion, he says: their God has sent him. Moreover, he adds that God has sent a communication to Pharaoh himself on the subject. The words are very abruptly given in the narrative; for however Moses himself might act the courtier, it did not become the Almighty even by his messenger to address the king in any cringing terms. So it was promptly and boldly uttered: "Thus saith the God of Israel, Let my people go."

Pharaoh was not accustomed to this sort of handling by either gods or men. Was he not "brother of the gods" himself? Who was it dare give him an order like that? Who was this Hebrew deity that assumed to control an Egyptian king? And Pharaoh said, "Who is Jehovah? I know not Jehovah, neither will I let Israel go." Ex. v. 2.

Moses in respectful language ventures a little urgency. He asks but for a brief holiday. The festival will only continue three days. It is not a very large allowance for men who have done the king such good service. But the king will have nothing to do with it. The abrupt demand of the Hebrew God has affronted him, and he turns upon the company of the chieftains and accuses them of hindering the people from their appointed tasks. "Get you to your burdens," he cries, and the interview is closed.

Not very encouraging, this, and they seem to have been surprised by it. God had indeed forewarned them to expect something of the sort (Ex. iii. 19), but the ready reception he had met among his own people seems to have driven the warning out of Moses' mind. A very unhappy termination was it to his visit at court, and there may have been some sneering among the courtiers as the Hebrews passed out.

XII.

WORSE AND WORSE.

THE principal work exacted of the Hebrews by the Egyptians was brick-making. It was once supposed that the great pyramids were erected by them, but the Scriptures represent them rather as building cities. Moreover, the principal pyramids are of stone, and there is no evidence that stone-work constituted any part of their tasks. Besides, the pyramids are of much more ancient date than the sojourn in Egypt, and may have been among the curious objects which caught the eye of Abraham.

The bricks they made were formed from the Nile mud, which, not being of itself sufficiently cohesive for the purpose, needed toughening by some kind of fibre. In modern times the plaster on the walls of houses is made firm by mingling hair with it. The fibre used for these bricks was straw, and bricks toughened with straw are still made in that country. They are not burned, of course, else the straw would be destroyed, but are dried in the sun, and in so dry a climate bricks made in that way endure for centuries. Such bricks are found to-day among the most ancient relics of that ancient land.* Upon a tomb at Thebes is a painting representing captives engaged in brick-making, the laborers being distinguished from their task-masters by their color. The painting is supposed to be of an age not far from that of Moses.

The exactions laid upon the Hebrews in this service were very oppressive. Even before the interview with Pharaoh, they had everything they could bear, but after that the policy seemed to be to make things worse and worse. Tyrants

* Hawks' Egypt, page 191.

BRICK-MAKING IN EGYPT.

sometimes introduce a vein of grim humor into their enormities, and it would almost seem as if Pharaoh undertook to play off upon these people a cruel jest. He virtually says that he is afraid they have not work enough. They must be quite at leisure, to be talking of going out for a three days' festival. Men seek amusements mostly to pass away time. He will furnish them entertainment nearer by. It is a pity to have time hang so heavily on their hands—they shall have something to do. "Ye are idle! Ye are idle! Therefore ye say, Let us go and sacrifice unto our God. Let more work be laid upon them." Ex. v. 8.

The special method which he took to increase their tasks was to require them hereafter, in brick-making, to furnish their own straw. Hitherto this had been provided by the government. Now they must supply themselves, and yet they must bring out the same daily rate of brick per man, or feel the lash.

The "taskmasters" who were to enforce this regulation were Egyptians. The "officers" under them were Hebrews, probably of the elders of the people. And the taskmasters hastened the officers and the officers the people, till at last all the ordinary supplies of straw were exhausted, and still the brick-making was driven on. As a last resort the people went out into the stubble-fields and undertook to secure some scant supply there, but it did not avail. They lost time in gathering straw and their tasks were behind; and when the officers reported the deficiency to the taskmasters, they laid upon them the bastinado, expecting them to whip the people in their turn.

Instead of that, the officers carried the case to Pharaoh. They doubted the authority of these taskmasters. They suspected that these new exactions had never been ordered by the king, or if they had been ordered, they believed that the time had come for a remonstrance, so they came up and made their complaint. But the king was still facetious; and affecting to believe that the people only needed more work, he said again, "Ye are idle! Ye are idle! There shall no straw be given you."

When the officers came back with this report, the people rose against Moses and Aaron. This is what comes of interfering, they said. If we had been let alone, we should at least have had straw to make our brick. "The Lord look upon you, Moses and Aaron! Ye have made our savor to be abhorred in the eyes of Pharaoh."

THE BASTINADO.

So it grew worse and worse. It seemed as if the old experience of forty years ago were going to repeat itself, and Moses' undertaking were again to prove a failure. The man was terribly shaken. He turned to God in his great bitterness and told him all. Familiarly, as was his wont—almost irreverently, as it may seem to us—Moses talked with God: "Lord, wherefore hast thou so evil-entreated this people? Why is it that thou hast sent me? For since the day I came to Pharaoh to speak in thy name, he hath done evil unto this people; neither hast thou delivered them at all."

If these words were irreverent, God forgave the sin, for his servant was sorely tried. And Moses in his turn forgave the people, for they also were sorely tried.

Here let us for a moment pause. The plot is thickening; the thunder-clouds are gathering in that silent Egyptian air. Man's extremity is God's opportunity; and soon a storm will burst upon that land which will rock the whole empire, release those bondmen and hurl proud Pharaoh from his throne. Wait on the Lord. Be of good courage, and he shall strengthen thine heart. Wait, I say, on the Lord. Ps. xxvii. 14.

XIII.

THE MYSTERIOUS NAME.

THE gods of Egypt each had a proper name. There were Amon and Apis and Phra; there were Osiris and Isis and Thoth, and so it went through the whole catalogue.* But with the Hebrew Deity it was otherwise. These oppressed people only claimed to have one God, and he was a God without a name. True, they had certain terms by which he was designated, but they were only such terms as were applied to other gods, and as were sometimes even applied to men. Or if they spake of him by the attributes which distinguished his nature, and called him "The Almighty" or "The Eternal," it yet remained true that they had for him no authentic proper name.

We are not informed whether this circumstance was ever the occasion of any embarrassment to the people or not. Among themselves everything was easily understood, but in such a land as Egypt, where gods were as numerous as men, there would be manifest convenience in giving to each deity a name. Moses felt this embar-

---

* Rawlinson's Herodotus, *passim.*

rassment, apparently, when first ordered down from the desert to deliver the people. Their ideas had become confused. Their sublime monotheism was enveloped by an atmosphere of polytheism. When he should say, "The God of your fathers has sent me unto you," they would be asking at once, "What is his name?" They would say to him, "We know of a great many gods down here in Egypt. Which one of them is our God? Or if ours is not one of these, who is he, that we may know him?"

This seemed a not unreasonable question, and Moses wanted to be able to answer it. So God announced a name by which he was willing to be known—a name that described his nature too: "Say unto them, I AM hath sent me unto you: I am that I AM. This is my name for ever, and this is my memorial to all generations."

In the sixth chapter of Exodus much the same things are repeated: "And God said unto Moses, I am JEHOVAH"—the word being essentially the same as that elsewhere translated I AM. Both words are derived from the Hebrew verb *to be*, and the designation given the Almighty in each case refers to his self-existence. So the term might have been rendered, "I am the Self-existent," or, "I am the Eternal." God was saying, "If you want a name by which to know me, I give you this: Call me JEHOVAH, the ETERNAL, the I AM."

Most of the gods of the ancients had some sort of parentage. Some were supposed to have sprung from the foam of the sea, others were earth-born, and others still sprang from other gods. But in giving himself the name Jehovah, God intended to say that he was a being underived and without parentage of any sort. He existed in the beginning, and he would exist to everlasting. He was a great God, and a great king above all gods. Ps. xcv. 3.

One circumstance on which there has been much discussion is that this name Jehovah is represented as something new: "I appeared unto Abraham and unto Isaac and unto Jacob by (my name of) God Almighty, but by the name Jehovah I was not known unto them." Ex. vi. 3. Yet God is called Jehovah long before Abraham's day. The word occurs in some of the very earliest of the sacred writings (Gen. ii. 4), and sometimes not as a term used by the writer merely, but by the people of whom he writes. Abraham calls God Jehovah (Gen. xxii. 14), and so does Jacob. Gen xxxii. 9. How could God say, "By my name Jehovah was I not known"?

The answer is, the word was used, but it was not at that time a name. Abraham calls God Jehovah just as he calls him the Almighty, or just as he might have called him the Underived or the Eternal. The word designates something in the nature of God, and was therefore used as a designation of God himself. But it was not formally announced as his name. Now, however, that occasion has come for his taking a proper name, he sets apart that word for the purpose. If you want a name for your God, call him Jehovah: "This is my name for ever, and this is my memorial to all generations."

This name was made very sacred. When the law was proclaimed, he said, "Thou shalt not take the name of Jehovah, thy God, in vain." To use that name lightly, and especially to curse and swear by it when angry, was an awful irreverence to be punished with death. Lev. xxiv. 10–16. Very solemn were the people when they uttered this word. A fond parent would sometimes affectionately embody a syllable of it in the name he gave a dear child, but its sacredness grew upon them with advancing years. At last they quite ceased to utter it at all.* Even the priests, in reading the law, would substitute for it some enunciation esteemed less sacred; and if one of the people found a scrap of rubbish anywhere with that awful word upon it, he would pick it up and lay it carefully away. At last the pronunciation was lost, and it is one of the questions that divide Hebrew scholars to-day whether the word should be pronounced Jehovah or not. In the Septuagint translation of the Scriptures the term is avoided as much as possible, and our English translators substitute for it the word LORD in capitals, wherever it can be conveniently done.

It has many times been noticed how our Saviour assumes this name when he says, "Before Abraham was I am" (John viii. 58), even as he claims the attribute represented by it when he says, "I am Alpha and Omega, the beginning and the ending, which is and which was and which is to come." Rev. i. 8.

* This did not occur till after the captivity. The Moabite stone shows that the word was in use as late as 888 B. C. The awful mystery of the Tetragrammaton was a post-Babylonish peculiarity.— *Chancellor Crosby.*

XIV.

SENT ONCE MORE.

WE left Moses complaining of his want of success with Pharaoh. We left the people complaining that Moses' interference had only increased their distress, and we left Pharaoh himself hard, unrelenting, and apparently disposed to be facetious over the misfortunes of the poor victims whom he was crushing. We do not know how long affairs continued in this state, but in the midst of the darkness God appeared and said, "Now thou shalt see what I will do unto Pharaoh."

It was right after this that he announced his name Jehovah. It was at a similar period of discouragement before Moses came down from the desert that he said, "I AM hath sent you." These mysterious words were intended to inspire confidence. What is Pharaoh? one might have said; or, What are all his gods? Moses acts under the direction of the Eternal, the Underived, Jehovah, the I AM. There is also at this point a great renewing of promises, almost as if the sixth chapter of Exodus were a repetition of the third. There is the same mention of the solemn treaty stipulation into which God enters with Abraham, Isaac and Jacob. There is the same expression of the very tenderest sympathy with the suffering people. There is the same solemn assurance that the difficulties of the case will all be conquered and the people set free. There is the same command laid upon Moses to go directly to Pharaoh on the subject; and, alas! to complete the parallel, there is the same old objection on Moses' part that he is not a good talker, and therefore is not a suitable man for the undertaking. Ex. vi. 30.

At last, however, everything is ready for a new interview with Pharaoh, and once more they claim an audience with the king. They have come on the same errand again they say: "Thus saith the God of the Hebrews, Let my people go." Instead of refusing them as before, and driving them away, Pharaoh demands a miracle of them. They say that their God has sent them; let them give some proof of it.

Pharaoh knows all the tricks of the jugglers and necromancers, and if these Hebrews undertake to play off anything of that sort upon him, it shall fare hard with them. He will have his test applied on the spot; right there where they stand, and without any collusion or opportunity for preparation, he will have them give a sign that what they say is true.

So when they say, "Let my people go," he answers, "Show me a miracle." And having been previously instructed of God what to do in such an emergency, Aaron throws down his rod and it becomes a serpent. So immediate a response to his demand, and so clear a one, must have startled Pharaoh somewhat. Surely this Hebrew God hath sent these men, he would say, and he must be a mighty God. And then the question would rise whether his own gods could be made to do a miracle of the same kind.

Under some such feeling was it, probably, that he called in his "wise men and sorcerers and magicians." These were of the priestly caste, by whom the gods were supposed to manifest themselves among men, and he intends to balance the Hebrew miracle by one from his own people.

How much time he gives these magicians we do not know. That would be an important element with them. Neither do we know how carefully he watched or how carelessly he allowed opportunity for trick and deception on their part. We only know that when the test comes they meet it to his satisfaction; for as they cast down their rods they become serpents, for aught he can see, the same as the rod of Aaron had become.

Now, what was this? We meet it again and again in this story, and it reads very much as if all were reality. Did these magicians work miracles, or was their performance a mere feat of legerdemain?

On the supposition that they wrought miracles, several particulars deserve notice. One is that they were miracles, in each case, in imitation of what Moses or Aaron had done. Another is that the Hebrew miracles always keep the upper hand, as in the case of Aaron's rod swallowing up the other rods. And still another is that they were miracles in the same direction as those of Moses, and never opposite. They could never undo what he had done, but only do the same thing over again. If, therefore, we should admit that these were real miracles, we should yet be able to say that they were only such as magnified those of Moses and Aaron.

An additional circumstance, however, casts strong doubt on any such view of the case. These were miracles wrought in opposition to God, and of such miracles we have no account, neither would such an account be credible. Even the possessed with devils in our Saviour's time never wrought any miracles against God. The miracle is rigidly restricted to its office as the seal of a divine commission.

When, therefore, we know that the Egyptians were skilled in legerdemain,* and when we see, as we often do, what marvelous deceptions persons so skilled can play off, it is but fair to judge that these Egyptian miracles were a mere jugglery. It is true that the narrative reads very much as if the miracles were real, but good biblical scholars affirm that we are not confined to that supposition by the original language.* And the narrative itself describes how, after a few apparently successful imitations of what Moses and Aaron were doing, those jugglers gave over, and as if in alarm at what they saw in Moses exclaimed, "This is the finger of God!" Ex. viii. 19.

This interview with Pharaoh was as barren of results, apparently, as the former one had been. He was no more disposed to yield after he had witnessed a miracle than he was before, and the chief interest of this part of the narrative arises from an incidental remark in explanation of the king's great stubbornness: "The Lord hardened Pharaoh's heart." Ex. vii. 13.

* Hawks' Egypt, page 196. \hspace{2cm} * Bush, in Loc.

This strong expression is several times repeated in this story, and the apostle Paul brings it up in his letter to the Romans. Rom. ix. 18. Some have endeavored to relieve this statement of its difficulty by citing a passage in which it is said that Pharaoh hardened his own heart. Ex. viii. 15. But God's agency in the same process is emphatically affirmed. What did God do?

It would accord with the Hebrew idiom to say that God hardened Pharaoh's heart if he only withdrew from him and left him to hardness. This, therefore, we may assume that he did. He took from him those influences which once tended to soften him, and left him to himself.

A second supposition is that the judgments he sent upon him hardened his heart. After God had withdrawn from him, those judgments would cease to have any softening effect; he would only grow worse and worse under them. God knew this. He sent those judgments with that in mind. It was not expected that he would be softened by them. No such thing was designed. He was dealing with the man, not in a reformatory way, but in retribution.

A third supposition, allowable in the case, is that God sent hardness of heart upon Pharaoh as a punishment. This is sometimes threatened against men (2 Thess. ii. 11), and sometimes visited upon them. 1 Kings xxii. 20, 23. When men grow very determined in wickedness, God sometimes gives them over. When they oppose all good influences, he lets loose evil influences upon them. The sly deceivers whom he had held back are unchained, the tempters he would not allow to touch them are no longer restrained, and he pours upon them retributive judgments under which they only go from bad to worse. Thus God hardened Pharaoh's heart—thus, it is to be feared, many a man's heart is hardened. The man is given over; the defences about him are swept away; he is made an example of the righteous judgment of God.

XV.

THE RIVER PLAGUES.

ALL that has been done thus far, as between Israel and the Egyptians, has been like the mere skirmishing of two armies before the battle is joined. Now, however, we have arrived at a point where the cannonading begins, and we are to see ten successive charges made upon the enemy's works and ten fierce battles fought before we hear the shout of victory. In other words, we have come to the history of the ten plagues; and as these went in couples, we take up first the two connected with and proceeding from the river Nile.

It was not long after the second unsuccessful interview of Moses with Pharaoh that the order came to him to meet the proud monarch at another place and in quite another way: "Get thee unto Pharaoh in the morning. Behold, he goeth out unto the river." Ex. vii. 15. This was Pharaoh's hour of worship. He was going down to dip himself in the Nile. Moses was to meet him in the very act, and to smite the stream to which he was paying homage.

So as the royal cortege came down, Moses stood in the way and met them. "Jehovah, God of the Hebrews," he said, "hath sent me unto thee, saying, Let my people go." Then without deigning to wait for the answer, which he knew before it was spoken, he told the king that this message had been sent him more than once already, and that now, as he would not hearken, the Lord was about to visit the land with a dreadful plague. It was a plague that should fall upon the one great object in which they chiefly trusted. It should touch the very river in which the king was about to bathe, and from an object of reverence it should suddenly be changed to an object of utter loathing.

No sooner were these words uttered than Moses waved his wand toward the Nile, and in an instant it became blood. Pharaoh saw it; his attendants saw it — one red seething mass rolling on toward the sea. The king gave up his ablutions for that morning and hastened back to his palace. But as he passed, wherever he saw Nile water, whether in stream, canal or pool, it was turned to blood. Nay, the curse pursued him into the palace, and whether it were in a vessel of wood or vessel of stone, whenever he looked on any water from the Nile, it glared back upon him with red horror.

The plague is spoken of as extending over all the land of Egypt; and as all the inhabitants were dependent upon the Nile for water, the distress must have been very great. They contrived, indeed, to quench thirst by digging wells along the stream, but this did not remove the chief terror, which was the constant sight of blood. One of the valuable products of the river, moreover, was its fish. These constituted with many families their main dependence for food.* But under this plague the fish all died. And then, as the torrid sun of that land poured down upon the stream, it grew putrescent (Ex. vii. 18) and sent up an exhalation that carried loathing everywhere.

The affliction continued seven days. All the land felt it and knew how it came about. Everybody was saying, "This is the work of the Hebrew God." And as he had smitten old Nile himself, and none of their thousand divinities came to the rescue, they took a lesson in the doctrine that Jehovah was above all gods.

Nevertheless, the king did not relent. For a week he could supply himself with water without serious inconvenience, and so he waited for the plague to go by. To strengthen himself the more he brought in his magicians again, and they undertook to show how they, too, could change water to blood. It would have been more to the purpose if they had been able to turn blood to water, for then they might have removed the plague. But Pharaoh was easily satisfied with their performances, and so he refused to let the people go.

Some of these judgments upon Egypt seem to have been intended to express contempt. They

---

* Rawlinson's Herodotus, ii. 130.

were wrought in ways to induce such loathing. The objects by which they were administered were so insignificant or so mean. It was not merely a feeling of suffering which was induced, but a sense of shame.

To some extent such was the case with the next curse that came up upon them from the river Nile. Among the creatures that breed and spawn along those sedgy banks is the frog, and strangely enough this creature was admitted to the Egyptian pantheon and worshiped as a god.* They had a frog-headed god and a frog-headed goddess, and the frog was embalmed and honored with sepulture in the tombs at Thebes. In this circumstance perhaps lies the explanation of the fact that the next plague was a plague of frogs.

Before it was sent, however, Moses and Aaron went in once more to see the king. They went on the old errand, and predicted that unless he yielded to their request another plague would soon fall upon the land. "Thus saith the Lord," they said, "Let my people go, that they may serve me; and if thou refuse to let them go, behold, I will smite thy borders with frogs." Ex. viii. 1, 2.

* Kitto Scrip. Read. in Loc.

It would seem as if a man who had held out through the plague of blood would not be very easily frightened at a threatening like this, but when it came it was sufficiently serious. Pharaoh himself probably did not suffer much from the former plague. He could shut himself up in his palace, and what water he needed could be easily obtained. But when the frogs came, it was different. They came into the houses, and they cared no more for the king's house than for any other. They filled the oven excavations which the Egyptians were accustomed to make in the ground. They swarmed through the bed-chambers. They croaked out from the beds. They sprang into the kneading-troughs. They squatted on the king's table, glaring at him with ogre eyes as he sat down to meat. Ex. viii. 3.

The nervous terror which the people felt, meeting these croaking creatures everywhere, can to some degree be imagined. The king himself was overcome by it; and when he could endure it no longer, he sent for Moses and Aaron, and agreed that if they would take away the frogs they might take the people also. It was a great victory, but, after all, a barren one, for when the frogs disappeared he would not let the people go.

The removing of this curse was not sudden. The frogs did not betake themselves to the river, as might have been expected, but died in the houses, in the courts and in the fields, wherever they might be, and the people searched out their putrefying remains from underneath their floors and from all obscure places, and threw them into great heaps till the land stank. Ex. viii. 14.

Thus "upon their gods also the Lord executed judgments." Num. xxxiii. 4. And if any Egyptian's reverence for the frog-god outlived this experience, it must have been deep-rooted indeed. How much the plague did for Pharaoh may be judged by the record: "And when Pharaoh saw that there was respite, he hardened his heart, and hearkened not unto them, as the Lord had said." Ex. viii. 15.

XVI.

THE TWO INSECT PLAGUES.

WE have already caught a glimpse of the divine plan in the ten plagues. It was first to break down the stubborn will of Pharaoh. But it was also, secondly, to strike a blow at the religion of Egypt. Hence these judgments were so ordered as to smite the objects of their greatest reverence. The Egyptians denied not the existence of Jehovah. It was indeed a new name to them, yet they did not doubt there might be such a god; but, judging from the condition of the people who did him homage, they were not disposed to consider him a very important god. Their own deities seemed far mightier, and they were also numerous, while the Hebrew people had but one solitary divinity. So Egypt despised them and their God.

This feeling must be corrected. The Hebrew God must be exalted and all the gods of Egypt brought low. Jehovah must show himself as a great God—one above all the swarming divinities of the Egyptian pantheon, the one only living and true God.

The first two of these plagues, therefore, as already noticed, fell upon two leading divinities of that land. But when we come to the insect plagues, we are not so sure. The terms are a little obscure. Egyptian mythology is not perfectly understood, and it adds to the difficulty of the case with common readers that our translators have used the two unfortunate words, "flies" and "lice."

The insects called lice here were a species of

mosquito, a small black fly something like the gnat.* Those called flies were probably a species of black beetle. Whether the gnat was regarded as a sacred creature or not we are not informed; but of its power to plague, when coming in any great numbers and with any unusual voracity upon the half-naked inhabitants of that land, few of us will be inclined to indulge any serious doubt.

In regard to the beetle our information is more exact. It was a creature held in high estimation. Its statue was carved in stone. Other gods were represented as paying homage to it. It was a common figure on seals and ornaments; and as it was venerated when alive, so after death it often received an embalming.† These creatures, crawling up from their holes in the ground and appearing in any great numbers where men walked, would create great annoyance. They

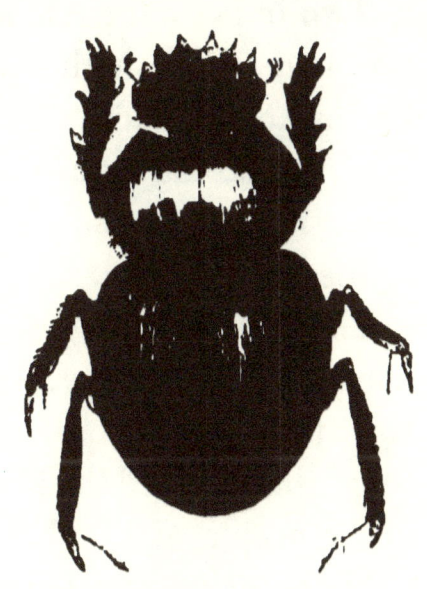

SCARABÆUS SACER.

* Hawks' Egypt, page 203.   † Kitto Scrip. Read. in loc.

must not step on one, and yet they crowded every highway and footpath. Swept from the floors, they instantly crawled back again. They climbed the tapestry; they covered the tables; they fell into every open vessel. They had an ugly fashion of eating into garments, and when too much disturbed of biting men. It was a plague that grew upon the people with the advancing days of its continuance, and under which king and people alike were sufferers.

Two important circumstances arrest our attention here. One is that at this point a distinction begins to be made with respect to these plagues between the Egyptians and the Hebrews. The other is that the magicians find their enchantments failing them.

The previous judgments seem to have fallen upon all alike. The Nile, that ran blood for the Egyptians, ran blood for the Hebrews also. The frogs, that plagued the idolaters, were also a plague to the people of the Lord. Probably there was a reason for it. Perhaps the Hebrews needed a lesson or two on the same doctrines that God was teaching the Egyptians. Quite likely they had learned to reverence these objects, and to attach to them a superstitious sacredness. Up to this point, therefore, it was well to make them partakers in the sufferings of their Egyptian neighbors. Now, however, the case is to be changed. Now God says to Pharaoh, "I will put a division between my people and thy people." Ex. viii. 23.

The failure of the magicians here is of vital moment. "The magicians did so with their enchantments to bring forth lice (gnats), and they could not." Why not? Is it any more difficult to bring forth gnats by miracle than to bring forth frogs? Nay, but it is more difficult to use such minute objects in legerdemain. Water and frogs could be handled, but to manipulate these little gnats, to carry them in a coat-sleeve, to shake them out when wanted and to make the people see them was not so easy. They were unsuited to any such operations; and being so small, all who inspected the process would be obliged to come very near, and that would expose the performers to detection.

Indeed, the magicians seem to be growing alarmed. The two Hebrew brothers wrought their wonders on so broad a scale as to throw all the petty performances of the Egyptians into the shade. They were ready enough for tricks, but these wonders began to assume an aspect of very grim reality. They wanted to retire from the field; they gave up the contest; they said to Pharaoh, "This is the finger of God." Ex. viii. 19.

Pharaoh was stubborn under the first of these two plagues, but when the second came he began to give way. Calling Moses and Aaron, he told them to go and hold their festival if they liked, but he said that it was not necessary to go three days' journey away to do it. They could celebrate just as well where they were. They answered, however, that such sacrifices as their God required were an abomination to Egyptians, and that the people would stone them if they saw what sacred animals they were killing to offer unto the Lord.

Among the animals which the Hebrews would offer were the ox, the cow, the sheep and the goat. All these were sacred in Egypt. Oxen, indeed, were sometimes sacrificed, but only such as had been very minutely examined by an Egyptian priest and pronounced suitable. Cows could not be sacrificed on any account, and in the locality where these events occurred both the sheep and the goat were in the same category.

To kill one of the sacred animals in that country always created great excitement. Diodorus relates an anecdote illustrating this point.

Some Romans were in Egypt on government business, and the Roman power was greatly feared there. But one of the party having unintentionally killed a cat, the people rose in a mob and set upon the unfortunate stranger, and not even the interference of the king himself could prevent them from putting him to death.†

Moses understood this feeling too well to undertake his festival where any Egyptians would behold them. "Shall we sacrifice the abominations of the Egyptians? Will they not stone us?" Pharaoh could not answer him. He did not undertake to do so. He knew the feeling of his people too well. So he merely said, "I will let you go that ye may sacrifice unto the Lord your God in the wilderness, only ye shall not go very far away. Entreat for me!" And Moses, after warning him not to deal deceitfully with them again, went out and entreated the Lord, and the plague was taken away.

Pharaoh's promise, however, was worth just as little as before. When he saw that the plague was removed, he would not let the people go.

* Hawks' Egypt, page 206.

XVII.

THE TWO PLAGUES OF PESTILENCE.

THE cannonading goes on two guns by two, the first each time unheeded and the second thus far bringing Pharaoh to terms. He made no promises for the plagues of blood, but when the frogs came he yielded. He would not bow his head for the gnats, but when the beetles came he said, "Go, sacrifice unto the Lord your God." Now two more blows are to fall, one upon the beasts of the land and the other on both beasts and men.

The new contest opens with the old formula: "Go in unto Pharaoh, and tell him, thus saith Jehovah, God of the Hebrews, Let my people go." Ex. ix. 1. Then follows the threatening: "If thou refuse to let them go, behold, the hand of the Lord is upon thy cattle." Moses enumerates the different sorts of cattle on which this plague shall fall. It will smite the oxen and the asses, the horses and the camels and the sheep. The meaning is that no sort of domestic animal shall escape. And that it may be seen to be no mere accident, the very day is set when the plague shall fall. "To-morrow the Lord shall do this thing in the land." Ex. ix. 5.

A plague upon the cattle of Egypt would touch the religion of the country as truly as the plague did which fell upon the Nile. Sacred animals were among the most common of the divinities of the land. When, therefore, a plague came that fell upon these creatures, a new class of their gods were hurled to the ground. In addition to this the visitation would involve great loss, for many people owned great property in cattle. Such was especially the case with Pharaoh, whose war-horses were so highly valued. Besides, there is something very distressing in the bare sight of great suffering among the lower animals; and as the plague went on, it is likely that their groanings and bleatings and howlings were heard on every hand.

Previous to the breaking out of this plague, God had promised to distinguish between the cattle of Israel and the cattle of Egypt, and Pharaoh was not a little curious to know whether such a distinction really existed. So he sent men out into Goshen who came back and reported that it was even so. While cattle of every sort were dying in Egypt, "behold, there was not one of the cattle of the Israelites that was dead." Ex. ix. 7. And yet the heart of Pharaoh was hardened, and he would not let the people go.

Then came pestilence in a different form: "And the Lord said unto Moses and unto Aaron, Take you handfuls of ashes of the furnace, and let Moses sprinkle it toward heaven, in the sight of Pharaoh. And it shall become small dust in all the land of Egypt, and shall be a boil, breaking out with blains upon man and upon beasts." Ex. viii. 8, 9.

This plague came without any previous argument. Pharaoh would not yield to the blow that had just been struck, so, without another word with him, a plague is sent upon both beasts and men. Those ashes bring it. They sift down in a sleet of fine dust all over the land, and whatever that dust touches, whether it be man or beast, breaks out in these itching, painful and offensive boils. It comes immediately. It lights upon the magicians before they have time to go out from the presence of the king. Pharaoh himself feels the sting, and his royal blood rankles in his veins.

Under this plague the magicians, who were of the priestly caste and stood as the representatives of the national religion, were smitten. Through them was it that men had access to the gods, and by them was it that the gods wrought their wonders among men. So when they were touched by the plague, another sacred place in Egypt was profaned. First on the gods themselves, then on their ministers—so fell the blow. And in this case the visitation was very severe. Yonder were the beasts; here were the men. These boils and blains were alike upon them all. The sacred beasts fared no better than the common beasts. The sacred men were visited the same as common men. And the case was the more marked because there stood Aaron and Moses, and there were the whole Hebrew people untouched by the plague. Surely it must by this time have seemed to the Egyptians that the Hebrew God was carrying affairs against them with a high hand.

And so it was; for it appears that the magicians, impressed with the awful visitation, had begun to remonstrate with the king, but "he hearkened not unto them." Moreover, it seems, from a subsequent notice (Ex. ix. 20), that there were some in Pharaoh's house that feared the Lord. These signs and wonders had been having their effect. Or perhaps these were people who had previously obtained some knowledge of God. At a court where such men as Joseph and Moses had once dwelt it might be a long time before the fragrance of the true religion entirely disappeared. So these believers at court joined with the magicians, and said, "Let the people go." But Pharaoh was unmoved. Possibly the suffering he endured enraged him. At any rate, he was as stubborn as ever, and would not let the people go.

XVIII.

THE PLAGUES UPON THE FRUITS OF THE EARTH.

IT has already been observed that the land of Egypt abounded in gods; and as these appeared conspicuously in the animal world, so were they also found in great numbers in the vegetable creation. They had their sacred plants as well as their sacred cattle, and it was not alone in the more beautiful of these objects that they found something to worship, but other plants came in for their share of the divine honors. Even the leek and the onion were set in this vegetable pantheon; and if the God of the Hebrews were to have a clear ascendency, there must come some plague upon the vegetable world.

The multiplicity of gods in Egypt requires an explanation. How could an Egyptian, a man advanced beyond most people of his age in general knowledge—how could such a man as he believe that an ox or a sheep was a god, or pay his devotions to a leek or an onion? The answer to this question runs back to the origin of Egyptian worship, and of this I know of no better account than that given by Prof. Charles Anthon, who refers it to what is known as Fetichism.*

The lowest type of religious thought existing among those tribes who have lost the knowledge of God, is that in which natural objects are supposed to be endowed with supernatural qualities.† A superstition somehow arises among such a people that to kill a certain bird brings "bad luck." This constitutes the bird a god—not indeed such a God as Jehovah, spiritual, eternal, for of such a God they have not even formed a conception. They have no notion of a god that stands any higher than the regarding of that bird with a superstitious feeling. And as they consider it an omen of evil to kill the

* Art. Egypt, Class. Dic. † Lecky, Morals, ii., page 112.

bird, so they expect some good to come of it if they show it any kind attention. They feed it; they reverence it; they at length salute it with words of objurgation or entreaty. This constitutes the worship they offer; and as a similar superstition attaches itself to some other bird or beast, the number of gods increases. Gradually the feeling extends to plants and trees. Some of them are sacred. Worn about the person, they serve as charms. They protect the wearer against disease; they ward off misfortune. And when the object itself cannot easily be obtained, an image is made of it, and the efficacy is supposed to reside in that. Such are the gods of certain tribes of rude and savage people.

This is Fetichism, and there are remains of it in the most Christian countries. One man carries a horse-chestnut in his pocket to protect him from rheumatism. Another shudders and apprehends a quarrel when he upsets the salt. A third is alarmed and looks for bad luck if he sees the new moon over his left shoulder. And for another it is an excellent omen for a cock to crow upon his doorstep. These superstitions, or others like them, are found everywhere. That they should appear among the Egyptians might naturally be expected, and without any counterbalancing revelation from God, such superstitions might well be supposed to hold the minds of even educated men with great power.

If, then, you ask whether the Egyptians believed an ox or a leek to be a god, the answer is, In the Christian sense of the term, no. They had not even an idea of such a God as the Christian religion reveals. But if the term be taken in the pagan sense, and especially in the sense of the paganism of a very low type, the answer is, Yes. The Egyptians regarded those objects as gods in the only sense in which the ruder class of Egyptians knew anything about a god. They were natural objects endowed with supernatural qualities. And if there were men among them whose ideas had become more advanced, it would be very easy to contrive from the old superstitions a system to meet their minds. What was at one stage reverenced as a kind of savage charm was in the next age exalted as a type of some force in nature. It was the same superstition holding the mind of the scholar that held that of the slave, only the scholar had invented a reason for it which he was less ashamed to avow. Hence we find, among the higher and lower classes in Egypt alike, a tendency to deify a great number of very common things. It was the old African Fetichism clinging to the empire amid the grandest civilization to which it attained, though perhaps mingling with and modified by some remaining traditions of the true religion coming down from the Noachic day.

The gods of the animal world have been smitten by the two plagues of pestilence. What help the Egyptians might have expected from that quarter had entirely failed them. The question remained, however, whether a country so famous for its vegetation could not produce something in that department, if no other, which should stay the devastating march of the Hebrew God. A broad realm was open here, and one much relied upon. Whatever else had been smitten, no plague had yet fallen upon the fruits of the earth. To this quarter, therefore, Jehovah now directed his avenging hand, and in two terrible blows smote every object on which an Egyptian could depend.

The first of these blows came in the shape of a hail-storm. The formula for climate in Egypt is, "In that country it never rains." But for Lower Egypt, with which we have principally to do in this narrative, that statement is not strictly true. It seldom rains there, and in no year is the fall of moisture sufficient for the purposes of vegetation. Still, rain is not entirely unknown,* and even a hail-storm sweeping across the Arabian Desert sometimes trails its skirts a little way down along the Nile.

Now, however, a storm was to burst upon the land the like of which had never been known there. It was to be a hail-storm attended by lightning and thunder. Such was to be its severity that no man could live through it without shelter. Even the cattle, if left in the open field, would be destroyed.

Moses gave warning of it. He told the king that it would come the very next day, and he advised the bringing in of the cattle to a place of shelter.

We make at this point the interesting discovery again that there are some in Pharaoh's house who fear the Lord. Such, it is said, "made their servants and their cattle flee into the houses; while he that regarded not the word of the Lord left his servants and his cattle in the open field." Ex. ix. 21.

The morrow, therefore, dawned. The appointed hour arrived. And God said unto Moses, "Stretch forth thy rod." He did so, and

* Hengstenberg, Egypt and Books of Moses, 12, 2.

on came the storm, mingling thunder, hail and fire. The fire was, of course, the lightning, and it ran along upon the ground, tearing up the very soil. It is said the hail was "very grievous," and the particulars are given of its breaking the tree-branches and smiting the herb of the field.

This was the seventh plague, the storm; and when Pharaoh heard the crash of the great hailstones on his roof, when he saw the lightnings flashing through the gloom, and when he listened to those mighty thunderings, always regarded in that day as the voice of the gods, he began to tremble. All his charms were failing him. Heaven and earth seemed crashing the one against the other.

He could endure it no longer. Sending for Moses and Aaron, he begins to cry, "I have sinned, I and my people. Entreat Jehovah that there be no more mighty thunderings and hail; and I will let you go, and ye shall stay no longer." Ex. ix. 28.

Moses, warned by past experience, had no confidence in this promise, but he acceded to Pharaoh's request; and "when he spread abroad his hands, the thunder and the hail ceased." And once more the record was made against the king that he had been false to his promise and would not let the people go.

One or two circumstances in this narrative help us to a date, and a date sometimes assists wonderfully in giving such an account an aspect of reality. The warning given to Pharaoh to bring in his cattle before the storm limits the time to the months of January, February, March and April; for it is only in those months that cattle in Egypt graze in the field. Owing to the peculiar climate of the country, they have to be supplied during the remainder of the year with dry fodder.*

Another statement made is that "the barley was in the ear and the flax was bolled; but the wheat and the rye were not smitten: for they were not grown up." Ex. ix. 31, 32. Barley and flax in that country are about a month in advance of wheat and rye, and would be in the condition described in February or early March. The wheat and rye would be in the blade at that time, but not "headed out," and so not susceptible to fatal injury from a hail-storm. We shall not miss the truth very far, therefore, if we say that the plague of the hail occurred about the first of March. The first plague of the series,

* Hawks' Egypt, page 209.

that upon the river Nile, occurred about the first of January, the last of the series came at Easter or in April, so that these successive tempests of divine wrath were occurring at intervals for about four months; and counting some time for the preliminary endeavors of Moses with Pharaoh, it is likely that he and Aaron came down from the desert in the previous autumn. The entire period of this controversy, therefore, was about six months—six strange, trying months to the Hebrew people, six terrible months to Pharaoh and his land.

The companion plague of the locusts followed that of the hail, and swept from the land what little had been left by the storm. It was preceded by a new demand and a forewarning: "How long wilt thou refuse to humble thyself before me? Let my people go." Ex. x. 3. Pharaoh would not have endured this kind of address when Moses first appeared before him, but he is becoming accustomed to it, and Moses is growing bolder. Moreover, Pharaoh's servants once more interfere, and the king perhaps apprehends some sharp opposition in his own house. His lords and princes begin to be clamorous. "Let the men go," they say. "Knowest thou not that Egypt is destroyed?" So he sent for Moses and Aaron and offered a compromise.

"I will let you go," said the crafty king, "but who shall go? You do not care to take your families, of course. Let the men go, and let the families remain."

Thus far not a word has been said to Pharaoh with reference to the emancipation of the Hebrews. The challenge "Let my people go" has only signified, Let them go out into the wilderness for the proposed holiday. But as the contest begins to assume those gigantic proportions which it has now attained, Pharaoh sees that something else is in contemplation. These great plagues are not brought upon the land with reference to a mere holiday matter; the movement is too grand; the agencies are on too broad a scale. This looks toward emancipation, and Pharaoh is resolved to prevent that at all hazards. This is what he means by offering to let the men go without their families. He will keep their wives and children as hostages for their return.

When this proposition is made, Moses is roused to indignation, and he answers, promptly, "We will go with our young and with our old, with our sons and with our daughters, with our flocks and our herds will we go." This throws down the gage of battle. Pharaoh understands what such words mean, and he will never consent to anything which looks toward emancipating these slaves. If they choose to go for a festival merely, well; only it must be distinctly understood that their families must stay behind. If they reject that offer, let them look to it. Their schemes are uncovered at last. "And they were driven out from Pharaoh's presence." Ex. x. 11.

THE LOCUST.

Then came the plague. Moses waved his wand and the east wind rose. Directly heavy clouds began to obscure the sun, and there was a strange murmuring in the air. "The locusts! the locusts!" cried out the people in alarm, and soon they began to light upon the ground. Still the east wind blew and the cloud grew dense, till the whole land was clothed in twilight. And on the ground how the fierce creatures covered the soil! They seized upon the grass; they ravaged the wheat-fields; they covered the trees; they climbed upon the houses; they dropped into the pools; and still on they came. Nothing would be left after such a plague passed by. Egypt would be as barren as before that wonderful valley was scooped out by the Nile.

Then Pharaoh called for Moses and Aaron in haste, and said: "I have sinned against Jehovah your God and against you. Now, therefore, forgive, I pray thee, my sin only this once, and entreat Jehovah your God that he may take away from me this death only." Moses, therefore, prayed again, when a strong west wind arose, which soon carried all the locusts into the sea. Then Pharaoh once more hardened his heart, and would not let the people go.

XIX.

DARKNESS AND DEATH.

WE feel ourselves drawing near the crisis in this "battle of the gods." The light skirmishing upon the outposts was past long ago. For some time we have been hearing the roar of heavy artillery. Now the reserves have come up, and the commander on the Hebrew side is saying, "Now thou shalt see what I will do unto Pharaoh." Four times has Egypt lowered her flag and sent in her offer of surrender. Four times has Pharaoh hung out his signal of distress, which Moses has answered in God's name by removing the plague under which the land was perishing. And on each occasion the faithless monarch has broken the truce as soon as relief has come. It is idle to yield to his entreaties any longer. It is folly to consume time in further demands upon him or expostulations with him. The man must be crushed. His power must be broken.

No new demands are made, therefore, no new interviews asked, before the next blow falls. The plague comes without even a forewarning. "And the Lord said unto Moses, Stretch out thy hand toward heaven, that there may be darkness over the land of Egypt, even darkness which may be felt. And Moses stretched forth his hand toward heaven, and there was thick darkness in all the land of Egypt three days. They saw not one another, neither rose any from his place for three days; but all the children of Israel had light in their dwellings." Ex. x. 12, 22.

This is the inspired description of the ninth plague. One easily conceives the horrors attendant upon it. Great darkness always carries with it a kind of terror, and this is the more especially true if it be darkness that comes at any

AMUN-RA.
The Egyptian Sun-god.

extraordinary time. Egypt, moreover, is a land of almost perpetual sunshine,* and any obscuration of the sky is unusual. What terror, then,

* Hawks, page 213.

must have seized the people when day was turned to night!

Besides, the heavenly luminaries were among the objects of their worship, the sun, of course, holding the chief rank. The sun-god, Amun-Ra, gave name to the No-Ammon of the Scriptures (Nahum iii. 8), Thebes of modern geography, his temples at that city being favorite resorts of the worshipers of this deity. When, therefore, the Egyptians saw clouds gathering in the sky, the sun hidden, twilight descending when it should have been high noon, and that twilight itself rapidly deepening to total darkness, it was as if they had come to the last day of time.

But it was not merely the darkness that affected them; along with it came a certain damp shivering sensation as strange in that dry climate as the darkness itself. If a lamp were lighted, it would either go out or burn but feebly in the misty air. No artificial means could dispel the gloom, and with none of our modern contrivances for measuring time, they could only guess how long the plague might be lasting. Day and night were all one. There was no sun; there were no stars. No one ventured abroad; no one could tell when the scene would end. It took the entire three days to bring Pharaoh to terms, and for aught he could judge the three days might have been as many weeks. "And Pharaoh called for Moses, and said, Go ye and serve the Lord, only let your flocks and herds be stayed. And Moses said, Our cattle shall also go with us. There shall not an hoof be left behind."

At this the king again took fire. So impracticable a man as Moses was not to be tolerated. He bade him begone. He threatened that if he ever came to the palace again on that business it should cost him dear. He had suffered himself to be bantered and browbeaten too long already. "Take heed to thyself. Thou shalt see my face no more. For in the day thou seest my face thou shalt die." Moses accepted the situation, and took up the challenge. The time for talking was at an end. "It is well," he answered. "Thou hast well spoken. I will see thy face no more."

It is noticed in this narrative that through all this darkness the children of Israel had light in their dwellings. Those three days, therefore, could be occupied by them in such a way as might best serve the occasion. They could not be kept at their brick-making at such a time, and indeed it may be questioned whether that kind of work had been going on very much at any time since the plagues began. Gradually their submission to their Egyptian lords would cease. More and more they would feel that their deliverance was drawing nigh, and under that feeling they would naturally gather for mutual consultation and busy themselves in arrangements for their departure.

The most of the time Moses and Aaron were among them. Their calls upon the king were not very frequent, nor did they consume much time. Many of the preparations needed for the exodus, therefore, could be accomplished under their direction, and when the crisis came they could move on the very shortest notice.

That crisis came with the plague of death. It was the death in one night of the first-born child of every Egyptian family. But that plague is so closely connected with the institution of the passover that its examination will more properly come up in a subsequent chapter. It was the companion plague of the darkness. It completed the number, ten. It was the last, the most crushing and the most effective blow under which Pharaoh and the Egyptians were smitten. "And it came to pass that at midnight the Lord smote all the first-born in the land of Egypt, from the first-born of Pharaoh that sat on the throne unto the first-born of the captive that was in the dungeon. And there was a great cry in Egypt." Ex. xii. 29, 30.

XX.

MAKING READY.

THE removing of a nation of two or three millions of people from Egypt to Palestine, even if there had been no opposition to contend with, was an herculean undertaking. To do it against the will of the reigning monarch of course required the most cautious arrangement of details and the most thorough organization of the tribes.

From the day that Moses and Aaron came down from the desert, therefore, it was kept before the people, and as rapidly as possible they were put in readiness for the wonderful movement. Each tribe knew its commander. Each commander knew his subordinates. Doubtless also the general direction of the march was understood, and from what point they were to start. And, as the plagues came on and their task-work ceased, each family would be busy in preparing for a sudden departure.

One thing which Moses had the people do at this time has been strongly objected against. It is recorded in the following passage: "And the children of Israel did according to the word of Moses, and they borrowed of the Egyptians jewels of silver and jewels of gold and raiment." Ex. xii. 35. These things they never returned.

EGYPTIAN WOMEN AND THEIR JEWELS.

What they "borrowed" in this way they carried with them out of the country. Some suppose that it was never their intention to return these things, and in that light the case looks very much like a fraud.

But whatever the nature of the transaction would have been in ordinary circumstances, in this case we are to remember that it was commanded of God. It was not a thing that Moses contrived, but a procedure directed entirely by a divine revelation. This alone would take it out of the ordinary range of right and wrong.

Besides, when we come to examine this "borrowing" very closely, there is nothing in it implying any pledge of repayment. The word translated "borrow" is the same which, in Ps. cxxii. 6, is translated "pray." Pray for the peace of Jerusalem, says the psalmist. Pray for the jewels of the Egyptians, says Moses. There is no pledge of returning anything implied in the term. If we read the passage with the word ask instead of borrow, we shall have the whole truth. They asked these jewels and this raiment, and the Egyptians gave both.

Some of this jewelry might have been the property of the Israelites. Perhaps the Egyptians had borrowed it of them, and perhaps this asking for it was only calling in the loan, so as to be ready for the march at a moment's notice.

Or if it should still be insisted upon that the

borrowing was exactly what the English word "borrow" implies, then the circumstance is to be taken into account that the children of Israel perhaps did not know but they should come back into Egypt before they actually went to Palestine. They had been asking leave to go three days' journey into the wilderness to hold a religious festival. They knew, of course, that this was preparatory to their final exodus. But, so far as we know, they expected to come back from the festival and start in a more direct course for the promised land.

The jewels were borrowed for the festival. It was a custom of the times. When people went to do honor to the gods, they went in goodly apparel; and if they had it not of their own, their neighbors freely lent to them. They desired to appear joyfully before the gods, and to refuse to lend in such circumstances was supposed to incur the displeasure of Heaven. So perhaps the Israelites did borrow these jewels intending to return them. But when they had gone their three days' journey, they found that they could not go back. And as Pharaoh just then also made war upon them, this Egyptian property, according to the usage of the times, became their lawful prey. At any rate, "the Lord gave the people favor in the sight of the Egyptians, so that they gave unto them: and they spoiled the Egyptians." Ex. xii. 36.

One preliminary to their going was of vast significance. That was the instituting of the Passover, and this carries us back to the tenth plague.

When it was threatened that the first-born child in every Egyptian family should die, special directions were given to the Hebrews how to escape the visitation. On the night of the fourteenth of the month Nisan or Abib, which corresponds nearly to our April, God was "going out about midnight into the midst of Egypt" Ex. xi. 4) on this errand of death. And when he said he was "going out," it was as significant a threatening as when he said, "I am coming down." It meant that the business was to receive, in some high sense, his personal attention, and that it would be most thoroughly performed. Hitherto the difference he had put between his people and their oppressors had been effected without any precautions on their part. To escape the plague now coming, however, they must solemnly wait upon him, in accordance with the directions he was about to give.

The first of these directions was that they

must all be withindoors. Any Hebrew found abroad that night would perish. The next direction was that their doors should be marked, so as to show that the people within were Hebrews. Any family who should fail to mark their door would be visited as if they were Egyptians. The special direction concerning this door-mark was that it should be made with blood. This blood was to be sprinkled with a bunch of hyssop upon the lintel and the side-posts of the door. Moreover, it was specified what kind of blood this should be, and how they should obtain it. And here we reach the vital point of the arrangement.

Each family must kill a lamb. It must be a lamb carefully selected, and after its blood had been sprinkled the lamb itself must be roasted and eaten. When they gathered round the table to eat it, each one must be upon his feet ready for marching. They must all

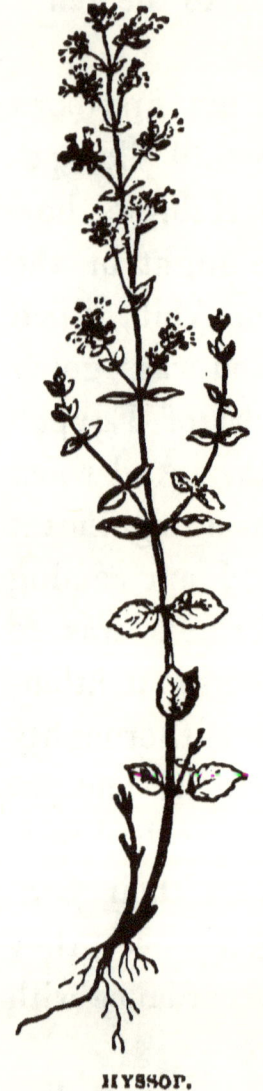

HYSSOP.

have their robes girded, their sandals on, and each man a staff in his hand. They must be careful not to break the least bone of the lamb; and if any of it were left after they had eaten, it must be burned.

Such was the sacrifice of the Passover—such was the solemn religious festival with which their stay in Egypt was to be concluded; and the observance instituted that night was to be repeated once each year through all their generations.

Looking at this festival in the light of the New Testament, we see in it a meaning of the most marked importance. It not only served to commemorate the deliverance from Egypt, but it foreshadowed a more marvelous deliverance provided for us all. That spotless lamb represented the Lamb of God, that blood on their doors signified his blood shed for sin, and that plague of death from which they were thus delivered represents the ruin into which guilt brings the soul. Our Saviour's crucifixion occurred exactly at this Passover season (Luke xxii. 5), and the apostle speaks of him as "Christ our Passover." 1 Cor. v. 7. To the patriotic Hebrew this festival was like our Independence day. To the more devout of that nation it revealed its deeper meaning, and carried the mind forward to the Great Sacrifice that should be made for the sins of the world.

The preparations therefore were all made, and the fourteenth of Nisan came and they killed the sacrificial lamb. This occurred "between the two evenings" (Ex. xii. 6, *margin*), or in the after part of the day, before it was quite sunset. At sunset the evening of the new day began. The men came in from their occupations. The doors were marked with blood and fast shut together. The lamb was put upon the fire to roast, and all the house, young and old, were awake, silent, waiting. Toward midnight the roast was ready, and the household, staffed and girded, stood round the table. Fathers, mothers, sons and daughters, down to the smallest of the children, all were there. It was at the full of the moon, and in that clear air the sky must have been very bright. There was no token of coming evil to be seen, but the Lord's people were in momentary expectation. The feast was concluding, and they stood a moment, waiting for a signal to go.

It came. A shriek!—one solitary cry of distress ringing out on the still night air. It was, perhaps, a woman's voice; and directly there was another. Then there were still others, and the cry rose to one awful chorus, and the chorus rose to one mighty crescendo of woe, till the wild

DEATH OF THE FIRST-BORN.

outwail burst all boundaries and rolled across the empire.

The children of Israel knew what that meant,

and stood silent, while the little children clung to their mothers, who folded them in their arms. The last blow had been struck. It fell upon the palace, and Pharaoh gazed upon the dead face of the heir to the throne. It fell upon the lords and nobles; it fell upon the priests and magicians; it fell upon the captive in the dungeon; it fell like a thunderbolt from that moonlit sky; "and there was not a house in which there was not one dead."

Now the work is done. Now it will never again need be said to Pharaoh, "Let my people go."

XXI.

FORWARD.

"NOW the sojourning of the children of Israel, who dwelt in Egypt, was four hundred and thirty years." Ex. xii. 40. Their sojourning where? Some say in Egypt itself. This opinion is ably defended by Professor Green of Princeton, N. J., in his "Pentateuch Vindicated."* Abraham had been told that his seed should "be a stranger in a land not theirs four hundred years." Gen. xv. 13. This "land

---

* Page 119.

not theirs," says Professor Green, "must have been Egypt."

But when the apostle Paul computes this time, he makes only about four hundred and thirty years from the instituting of circumcision to the giving of the law. Gal. iii. 17. So it is probable that the four hundred years mentioned above includes the whole space of time from Abraham to the exodus. During all that time the Hebrew people possessed no country. Even while they were in Palestine they moved about from place to place, strangers in the presence of the tribes that held the soil. If this reckoning be correct, their residence in Egypt was only about two hundred and fifteen years.

One of the difficulties which this supposition encounters is, that it does not seem to give time enough for their vast increase of numbers. They came into Egypt, by round reckoning, just seventy souls. Gen. xlvi. 27. They went out of Egypt with a force of six hundred thousand men, besides women and children; and as the men able to go out to war could not possibly have been more than one-fourth part of the whole number, there must have been in all at least two or three millions. This increase is enormous. The world has never witnessed anything like it. And yet any one who will take the trouble to make the reckoning will see that just such an increase might occur in the regular order of nature.

The human family is naturally capable of a far more rapid multiplication than we ever witness, and we are expressly informed that the increase of the Hebrew population in Egypt was extraordinary. Ex. i. 7. Reckoning the bearing age of their women only from twenty to fifty, and reckoning to each woman of that age but one child for every two years, we easily make out the requisite number. At that rate of increase, far more than the three million would be found living at the end of two hundred and fifteen years.

Whether the time were longer or shorter, however, the day had come at last when they were to depart. It was well that everything was ready, for Pharaoh " called for Moses and Aaron that night and said, Rise up, and get you forth from among my people, both ye and the children of Israel, and go, serve the Lord as ye have said. Also take your flocks and your herds as ye have said, and begone; and bless me also. And the Egyptians were urgent upon the people that they might send them out of the land in haste:

for they said, We be all dead men." Ex. xii. 31, 32.

These successive judgment strokes had at length thoroughly aroused the Egyptian people. There was something like a panic among them, as indeed there well might be. They were not willing to have those Hebrews among them another day; and had Pharaoh undertaken to set himself against their going, the rising tide would have swept him from his throne. He was wiser than to attempt such a thing. He felt very much as the people did. He asked no hostages, had nothing to say about the leaving of the flocks and the cattle, but was simply urgent to get them away without further waiting. He does not, indeed, in terms emancipate them; he only says, " Go, serve the Lord, as ye have said ;" but that fiction of a three days' festival only covers his humiliation a little, and it quite offsets that to hear him begging their prayers and saying, " Bless me also." Ex. xii. 37.

So they formed in line and prepared to march. The head of the column was at Rameses. The direction in which they moved was to the east of south. This was not the road to Palestine, but to the wilderness, as they had said. The caravan increased as they went on. The pastoral portion of the nation occupied that part of the country through which they were passing; and being all ready for the movement, they fell into line, driving their flocks and herds with them as the column moved on. A mixed multitude also went up with them, some of them partly Egyptian and partly Hebrew—low-caste people who became a kind of camp-followers, adding to their numbers without doing them any good. In some cases the women were just making ready to bake bread when the caravan came along; and hastily rolling up the dough in a species of sack called a kneading-trough, they flung it over their shoulders and went on. Mostly they were on foot, though some of the little children might have found places on the camels and the asses. But they were a hardy race, inured to toil, capable of sustaining great fatigue, and "not one feeble person among their tribes." Ps. cv. 37.

They went up "harnessed" (Ex. xiii. 18), says the record. The margin renders the term "five in a rank." The Hebrew word involves the number five in some way, but it can scarcely mean five abreast, for arranged in that way the column would have been three hundred miles long. All we can certainly gather from the expression is that they were in some way arranged in regular army-like array, and that they did not rush out of the country a confused and disorderly rabble. It was an organized movement, arranged, no doubt, by a vast amount of previous work on the part of Moses and Aaron. How well the organization was effected we easily judge by the progress the mighty column made each day, and by the authority the chief leader was able to exercise along the whole line.

As they started from Rameses there suddenly shot up at the head of the column an immense pillar of bright cloud. It was a very early morning hour, probably some time before daylight, but this pillar sent back a line of brightness to the hindermost rank of the moving caravan, and as daylight came on its brightness faded and it trailed a welcome shadow along their path. On it moved, slowly, just in advance of them, guiding the way. By day its huge shadow sheltered the whole host; by night it flamed like a meteor against the sky. When it moved, they moved; when it halted, they halted. Sometimes they called it God's angel. Ex. xiv. 19. At other times they spake of it as God's presence. Ex. xxxiii. 14. At still other times they gave it the mysterious name which God himself had chosen, and called it Jehovah the Lord. Ex. xiv. 24.

It was one form of the Shekinah, the supernatural light by which God manifested himself to his people in those times. It was one of those ancient types and shadows the reality of which is found in our Lord and Saviour Jesus Christ. John i. 7–9.

Under this strange pilotage on they marched. Having so early a start, and withal being in high spirits and stimulated by the urgency of the Egyptians, they made a distance that day of something like twenty miles. This reckoning is for the head of the column. Many of the families and nearly all the droves of cattle fell in with the caravan farther down the country; and taking a position in the rear, they would make a very easy day's travel. When they encamped at night, they covered an area of nearly three miles square.

Their first camping-place was named Succoth. It was not a city, nor perhaps had it so much as a name till they gave it one. It was a mere halting-place among the groves of tamarisk and palm.* The word Succoth refers to the booths or huts of bushes under which they lodged for the night.

Some of the families, particularly such as were

---

* Stanley's Jewish Church, page 138.

keepers of cattle, would be provided with tents; but they had largely become an agricultural people in Egypt, and had lately dwelt in houses. They understood the art of manufacturing tents, however, and the spinning of goats' hair and the weaving of cloth for that purpose probably occu-

EGYPTIAN SPINNING AND WEAVING.

pied the women at their various halting-places. So, at a later day, and in the desert, we find them dwelling in tents, but for this first night out most of them were content to cut down branches of thick trees, and extemporize a shelter for the occasion.

As this was their first night out, so was it the last place for the present where they could cut down a great many tree branches; and the whole

* In the tombs at Beni Hassan, among other interesting representations of Egyptian arts and manners, we find paintings representing flax-dressers, with spinners and weavers engaged in the production of cloth.

scene was one calculated to make a vivid impression on their minds. This, therefore, rather than any other of their numerous haltings, was selected for commemoration after they should be settled in their own land. Lev. xxiii. 40. It was a pleasant camping, with that bright full moon shining through their leafy shelter, and for the most of them the fatigues of the day had only been such as to give a good night's rest.

The second camping-place was Etham, perhaps ten miles farther on, at the "edge of the wilderness."

XXII.

PURSUIT.

THE country through which they took their way presented great variety within a short space of travel. They went out from the most fertile region on the face of the earth; in three days they were in a desert. They left the low flat lands of the Delta; in three days they were among the sand-hills and rocky promontories that skirt the Red Sea. They took leave of the last city at Rameses; they took leave of the groves and villages at Succoth. The green country of

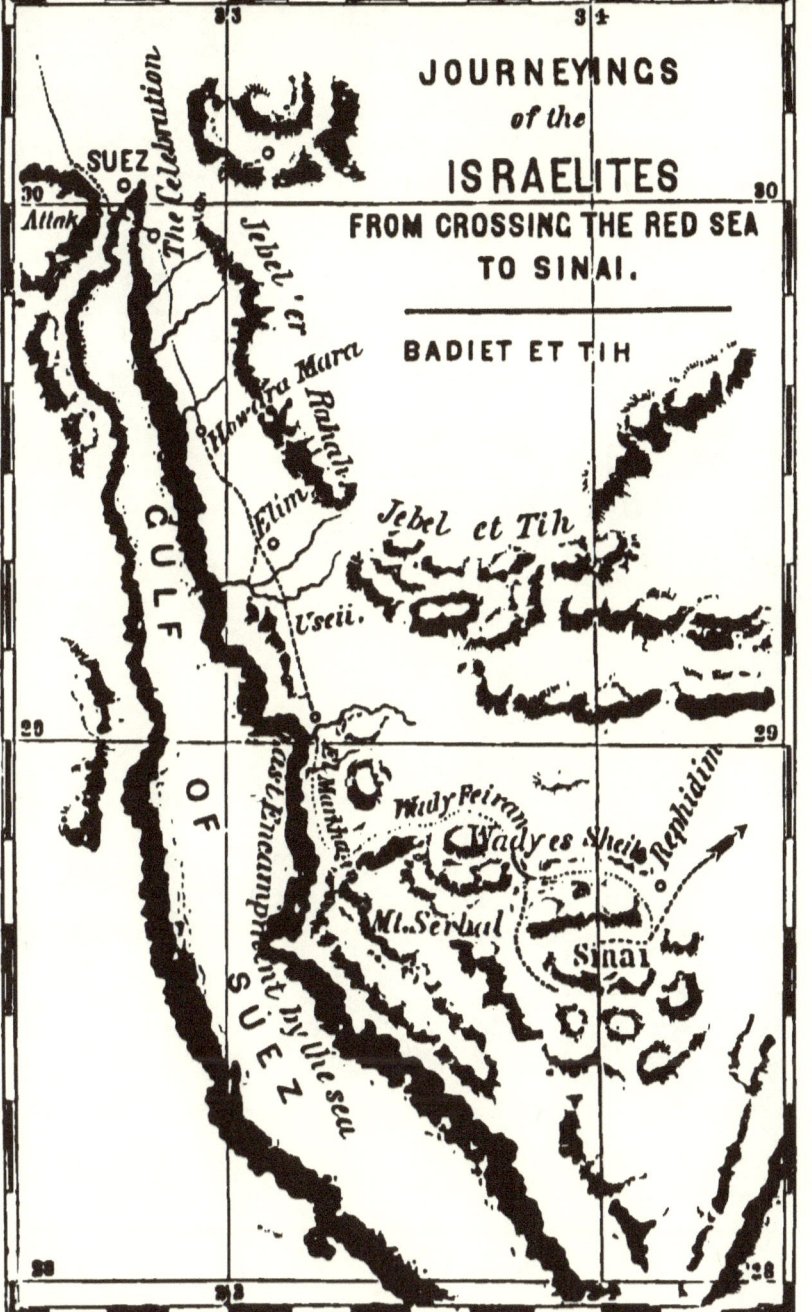

Egypt ceased at their second camping-place, Etham.*

Yet the green was not cut off by a perfectly even line. As the sea reaches long arms inland, so the desert ran in some places in barren strips of country toward the Nile; and as the shore-land shoots out into the sea in capes, peninsulas and promontories, so the fertile soil ran in some places in long green strips out among the yellow sand. The desert had its islands, too, moist places where pasture grew, and where they could repose a while in the shadow of the palm.

Still, at Etham, they made the transition, and from that point the desert features of the country more and more predominated. Around them were great wastes of coarse gravel. In marching they were often among the sand-hills. In certain directions they would pass a low growth of the desert thorn.

Another circumstance which marked the encampment at Etham was that, when morning dawned there, it was their third day out. This was important. They had asked leave to make a three days' journey to hold a feast in the wilderness. By a very close construction this could be called a three days' journey; and as for the

* Stanley's Jewish Church, page 139.

wilderness, it was all about them. What would they now do? If they made immediate preparation for the festival, well; if they moved on, Pharaoh might say they had broken faith with him.

Pharaoh was more than suspicious that they intended to move on. The narrative shows that he had his scouts out hovering about the camp to bring him word. It was a critical moment, and the issue was brought on by a new interposition of God: "And the Lord spake unto Moses, saying, Speak to the children of Israel that they turn and encamp before Pi-hahiroth, between Migdol and the sea." Ex. xiv. 1, 2. This was their marching order. They were not to stop yet for the festival. God was bidding them go on.

The direction to turn signified that their course was to be changed by a sharp movement toward the right. From Succoth they had been bearing to the south of east; now they must go directly southward, keeping in the direction of the western shore of the Red Sea.

What was the object of that? If they were going to run off to Palestine, they should have turned exactly the other way, and by a sharp flank movement to the left have pushed eastward and northward. Even if they wanted to go to Horeb by the way, their course did not lie down the west side of the sea, but they should have gone round the head of the gulf to pass down on the opposite shore. What means this unaccountable order? Even Moses might have found it difficult to answer that question, but in the light of subsequent events it is quite plain. It was one of the cases in which

> "God moves in a mysterious way
> His wonders to perform."

This movement is reported to Pharaoh, and he takes heart. According to his construction, they have broken their bargain with him. If they had stopped and offered sacrifices on that third day, he would have been content. But they are going on, running away, and by some infatuation they have missed their course, as he believes, and are now entangling themselves where he can easily catch them. Perhaps at last their God is deserting them. Perhaps at last the gods of Egypt are bestirring themselves. At any rate, it will be easy overtaking them and bringing them all back.

Pharaoh's military force must have been somewhat reduced by this time. So far as horses were concerned, at any rate, between the plague of pestilence and the plague of the hail, there must have been very few left. It was only a very meagre chariot force, therefore, that he could send against them, though, as the event showed, one quite sufficient to terrify them into the most abject submission to his demands. We read that "he took six hundred chariots and all the chariots of Egypt." The word *and* should read *even*. These six hundred were all the chariots he could muster for want of horses. The "horsemen" spoken of farther on were not cavalry, as might be supposed, for Egypt had no cavalry. The horsemen and the chariots were the same.

Six hundred chariots, however, would seem quite a force, and one day's hard riding would bring them up with the rear of the Hebrew column.

The caravan was toiling still slowly southward. Soon after leaving Etham they began to see on the left the green waters of the Gulf of Suez, then probably extending farther northward than now. From certain elevations reached in the march, they commanded a view of the entire valley in which lay this long arm of the Red Sea. It was much like the Nile valley in form —a deep cleft in the underlying rock—but it

AN EGYPTIAN CHARIOT.

was the Nile valley without its rich dress of green.* Nothing could be more desolate than the shores washed by those waters.

Soon they saw on their right a grand mountain-range. This was Jebel Attaka; and running in from the north-west, it directly shut them off from Egypt. The range showed a great profusion of brown peaks and gloomy hollows, and cut in a sharp serrated line against the clear sky.†

Still toiling on, this range began to crowd upon their path. When they had reached a point opposite the modern city of Suez, there was a space of but six or eight miles between this mountain and the sea. Then the range turned suddenly southward, leaving an open plain along the shore. This plain constituted their highway, and they pressed on over its hard gravelly surface, with the mountain on the right and the sea on the left. At last, a little below Suez, the range swept round in a semicircle of precipitous rock, leaving no sufficient pass for such a caravan farther in that direction. Thus their passage was effectually blocked. They were "entangled in the wilderness. The mountains had shut them in."

* Robinson's Researches, i., page 69.   † Bonar.

This was the trap into which Pharaoh saw them going. His army had followed their trail down along the shore, and now came in behind them, completely cutting off their retreat. It was nearly night when he came up with them; and as he had them shut in beyond all possible escape, all he had to do was to station his chariot force and go into camp till morning. Never was a tyrant more certain of his prey. Never were fugitives more handsomely caught.

XXIII.

A NIGHT TO BE REMEMBERED.

THE Hebrews, of course, immensely outnumbered the Egyptians, but they had no thought of resisting them. Their pursuers came in military array, and not only so, but in that terrible chariot array which in those days always struck terror into the minds of unarmed men. Six hundred chariots, small as the force would seem, was sufficient to cut its way through and through their camp, and to drive them, like flocks of sheep, whither the commander pleased. Chariots could be successfully resisted only by opposing chariots. Those throngs of men, women and children could never for a moment stop their course or stand before them.

It is not strange, therefore, that the Hebrews were alarmed when they discovered that Pharaoh was in pursuit.

Yet it cannot be denied that they behaved very badly. Scarcely three days had gone by since they left Egypt, where they had seen this same Pharaoh whipped into submission under the scourge of the ten plagues. All along they had been guided by the pillar of cloud and of fire, so that they could not suppose that they had mistaken their way. Even now that pillar was beginning to gleam on their camp, as evening came on, like a flaming sword uplifted by the almighty Hand. How strange that these six hundred chariots should eclipse to their minds all these visions of the almighty power of Israel's God!

But so it was. Long cringing under the lash, they knew not how to rouse themselves against their cruel masters. The oppressions they had suffered had unmanned them, and in their conduct on this first occasion of their falling into trouble, we see a good reason why God did not take them into Palestine by the more direct route, where they would have met with other enemies wielding war chariots. Their courage had all been beaten out of them, and no sooner was the Egyptian force in sight than they gave up everything for lost. "And they said unto Moses, Because there were no graves in Egypt, hast thou taken us away to die in the wilderness? Wherefore hast thou dealt thus with us? Is not this the word which we did tell thee in Egypt, saying, Let us alone, that we may serve the Egyptians?" Ex. xiv. 11. So they raged. It was very shameful, especially as it took the direction of personal hostility against Moses. The insulting words were not spoken by the mere rabble; these were the accusations of the chieftains of the tribes. From the least unto the greatest they were a people without any stable faith in God, and in the awful emergency Moses was obliged to stand quite alone.

He calmly breasted the storm. "Fear not," he says. "Stand still—stand firm*—and see the salvation of the Lord. The Lord shall fight for you, and ye shall hold your peace. Those Egyptians whom ye have seen to-day ye shall see no more."

He ceases speaking, and there is a new phenomenon at the head of the column. The pillar

---

* Bush, *in loc.*

of fire is lifting itself up and rapidly passing toward the rear. They look up and see it moving like a meteor along the darkened sky. Directly it settles down again, only now between the Hebrews and the Egyptians. Toward the latter it turned a dark side* (Ex. xiv. 20), so that they did not observe it, or perhaps they were sleeping. Soon it enveloped their camp like a cloud, but it still had a bright side for the Hebrews.

Meanwhile an east wind rises; and though an east wind there is usually a clear wind, the whole sky is thickly overcast. The sea is driven in furiously against the shore. Everything portends some grand event, and under these impressive influences the murmuring of the people has subsided and their fear has been changed to immediate expectation.

As the Hebrews gaze on the awful scene, Moses, standing perhaps upon a projecting rock, his form illuminated by the strange light that shines from the pillar of fire, lifts on high his wonder working rod and smites the raging waters. As the blow falls he gives the word, "Forward!" And at that word the waves are cut sharp asunder, as if by the very fierceness

---

* See Murphy, *in loc.*

of the wind, and the great host, all ready, move down, every man straight before him, into the broad open channel.

It is a strange path they walk, the crested waves standing in a wall of green crystal on either hand, but on they go, men, women, children, cattle, down among the wet sands, out among the coral groves, clambering over the rocks slippery with sea-weed, on, on, the meteor light streaming on their way from the rear, the rain pouring, the thunder crashing and the lightning leaping across the black sky.* Ps. lxxvii. 15–20. It was like a fearful dream. How they ever got through, they themselves perhaps could never tell, but by the first light of morning they were all safe on the opposite shore.

Pharaoh pursued them. How dare he do it? This question has exercised some minds with anxiety. Probably, however, he had no idea where they were going. We are to remember the darkness of the night, made still more dense to the Egyptians by the pillar of cloud. We are to remember that Pharaoh had no guide by which to pursue them except the sounds he might hear from their moving column, and that these sounds were heard amid the confusion of a

* See Alexander, *in loc.*

terrible storm.* Putting all these things together, it would not be an irrational supposition that he should imagine them endeavoring to file past his encampment; and that, waking suddenly in the night, he and his army should have quite lost their bearings, and have had no clear idea in what direction they were moving. Besides, he would easily persuade himself that he could go as far in the seaward direction as the Hebrews, and he had probably no idea of the miracle of the dividing of the waters.

At any rate, on he went. The ground was a little moist, but that would be accounted for by the rain. Now and then a chariot ran against a rock,† but rocks were to be expected along that shore, and this was one of the rough incidents of war. Soon, however, these mishaps began to multiply. The chariot wheels came off, the axles broke, the horses floundered, the men were thrown upon the ground, and at last the idea flashed across their minds that once more the gods were against them. Oh for morning! Never did tired soldiers more anxiously look for the dawning of the day.

At last it came. Day rises suddenly in those parts; and as the sun rose and the clouds swept

---

* Murphy's Exodus, page 154. † Murphy, ibid.

away, what a consternation! At first sight they could not perfectly take in the situation. On a second view pale horror was depicted on their faces. Brave men must not give way in great emergencies, however, and they reined their chariot horses to return to the shore. It was not more than five miles distant, and a half hour's hard driving would perhaps save them. But nothing is so difficult as to keep an army in good order while it is on a rapid retreat, and one sees them breaking ranks, falling into confusion, and soon each one caring only for his own safety. Moses saw their movement from the eastern shore; and when he once more lifted his rod on high, down thundered the heaped-up waters. Not a man escaped. Pharaoh himself perished among his chariots, and they were all "drowned in the depths of the sea." And "the Lord saved Israel that day out of the hand of the Egyptians; and Israel saw the Egyptians dead upon the seashore." Ex. xiv. 30.

The route by which we have endeavored to follow the children of Israel thus far is determined upon the supposition that Rameses, whence they started, was considerably north of the position which some assign it. It was once the custom to regard Rameses as identical with

Heliopolis or On, and the opinion prevailed for a long time that the Israelites marched from that point directly eastward to the sea, being hemmed in on each side by a mountain. There is a valley which might have been followed in this direction, and even Josephus falls in with the common view that this valley constituted their highway. This theory is based upon the supposition that they started from Heliopolis or On, near where the city of Cairo now stands.

The route which has been assumed as correct in this narrative places their starting-point not far from the ancient Zoan. The Scripture story obviously implies that Rameses, their headquarters, was close by the place where the miracles which brought the ten plagues were performed. These were "in the field of Zoan," mentioned in the eighty-eighth Psalm, and this Zoan happens to be one of the ancient cities of Egypt, the site of which is well known.* Its ruins are still very conspicuous in Lower Egypt, not far from the Mediterranean Sea, and just east of the Tanitic branch of the Nile. Zoan was a very ancient city and a very important one, and for that reason gave its name to the surrounding region, which was called the Zoan country, or the field of

† Smith's Dic.

Zoan. Rameses was in this Zoan country. Heliopolis was farther south. Most of our modern maps, therefore, locate Rameses not far from the Tanitic branch of the Nile and about halfway between Heliopolis and Zoan.

Dr. Robinson[*] labors hard to show that the point where they crossed the sea was where the modern city of Suez stands. This would not agree, however, with the statement that they were tangled in the wilderness, or that the wilderness had shut them in. At Suez the way of escape was open without their crossing the sea; but when they had been driven down the coast against Jebel Attaka, such was not the case. There they were completely entrapped.

Dr. Robinson seems to have sought this crossing at Suez to accommodate his theory of their making the passage at low tide. He does not understand that the waters were literally divided. The wind and the tide together, as he holds, laid open a path for them. This requires a more rapid movement on their part than is commonly assumed. The low tide at best would not serve them above three hours, and to move that host across in three hours we have to find a narrow crossing. At Suez the gulf is narrow, and

---

[*] Researches, i., 84.

that seems to answer the conditions of the occasion.

But the Scripture narrative says that the waters were divided. The sea went back all night. Ex. xiv. 21. The floods stood upright. The waters were a wall on their right hand and on their left. The low-tide theory is entirely gratuitous. The Bible makes no allusion to it, nor do the circumstances call for it. The passage of the sea was effected by a miracle.

At the point where we have supposed them to cross, the gulf is about ten miles wide.* This, as they ordinarily traveled, would be about a day's march. The same distance could have been made, of course, by marching all night; and if the channel were opened half a mile wide, they could pass over in twelve parallel columns, and so gain time. Twelve columns, each fifty men in rank, would have ample room in a breadth of half a mile, and no one of the columns need be above three miles long.

* Stanley, Sinai and Palestine, page 37.

XXIV.

THE GREAT AND TERRIBLE DESERT.

THE country into which the children of Israel passed by crossing the Red Sea is one of marked features. Some allusion to its peculiarities was made in Chapter VI. of this volume. It is now time to present it to our minds by a still more definite picture.

If we cast our eye upon a map of that region, we shall see in a direction due north the outlying range of Mount Lebanon. From this range, running southward through Palestine to the extremity of the peninsula of Sinai, we have what geologists would call a limestone country—that is, the upper stratum of rock, on which the soil rests, is limestone. Mount Lebanon on the north and the Sinaitic pinnacles on the south stand like watch-towers, overlooking this intervening region.

Underneath this limestone stratum lies one of sandstone, and underneath this is a stratum of granite. Long ages ago some subterranean force pushed upward from underneath these layers of rock, creating mountains. This force was most powerful just at the southern point of the Sinaitic peninsula; and as the mass was lifted, the limestone broke apart and the sandstone came through. With more lifting still the sandstone also parted, and the granite came through, shooting aloft into a great multitude of pinnacles and needle-like points that pierced the blue sky.* In approaching this higher region, therefore, one goes up from the level shore, among mountains of limestone formation. Beyond these he reaches a higher region, where the formation is sandstone. In the still remoter heights he finds himself amid the granite summits that are seen from afar. From these heights the great rifts or gullies, called wadys, go down in every direction toward the sea. These wadys are sometimes a mile wide, and often very deep, having been occasioned, in part at least, by the breaking open of the rock when the mountains were formed.

One of the special characteristics of this country is its drought. It is not absolutely a country where it never rains, for sometimes a winter storm tears across those heights with great violence, and pours down the wadys in an awful flood. But there is not rain sufficient for the purposes of vegetation, and storms of any sort are somewhat rare. The air is dry. The sky is

* Robinson's Researches, i., 113.

seldom obscured by vapor. The landscape is burnt and desolate.

Yet there are places where this desolation is relieved.* There are several points at which springs are found. One of these is in the vicinity of Horeb, well up in the granite interior, and wherever there are springs vegetation spreads on every hand. There are other places where the rock is hollowed into a species of natural reservoir, retaining the rain when it falls, and receiving the products of the torrents that pour in that direction during a storm. When these rock reservoirs are of granite, the water is very well kept,† and the vegetation that springs up in such a place forms an oasis. There are several such places on the peninsula —spots of delightful verdure amid surrounding desolation. And from all these sources sustenance is obtained even to this day for large herds of cattle and flocks of sheep. It only needs the touch of water at any point to make the desert grow green, and there is the very best evidence that in ancient times these green places were more numerous and more extensive than they are now. The trees and bushes that, at the time of the exodus, attracted the clouds and shaded

---

* Sinai and Palestine, page 17. † Bonar's Sinai, page 192.

the soil from the fierce sun, were cut away by the Egyptians when they were engaged in working the copper-mines of that country. And even to this day the process is going on, the Arabs cutting every shrub and tree that comes in their way to burn it into charcoal,* and the natural result is that each year the country is becoming more and more a waste.

Being a dry country, it is also a naked one. In our own part of the world even the most mountainous districts support a heavy growth of vegetation. On the peninsula of Sinai the earth stands bare; the mountains are naked rock; the plains and valleys are coarse hard gravel or drifting sand. As there is no vegetation, so there is no soil. Nothing covers the original ruggedness of the primitive formation. Every pinnacle, every cleft and seam and hollow, every break and contortion, stands revealed, and the pure air and powerful sunlight make everything strangely distinct. Those ragged rocky heights near the interior make up a scene of as terrific desolation as the world perhaps can show.

Another peculiarity of the country, manifest from the same cause, is the weird and unearthly

* Palmer's Exodus, page 194.

coloring that prevails.* Those massive mountains, so utterly stripped of covering, present the varieties of native rock of which they are formed in bold relief against that dazzling sky. Here is a great cliff, gleaming in the sunshine, white as snow. At its side rises another nearly as black as charcoal.† Not far away is a summit that glows in a bright red; farther on is one of green, and all varieties of brown appear, sometimes variegated with broad stripes of purple running from the summit of the mountain to its base, appearing precisely as if painted there by the hand of man. These strange colors intermingling, the effect heightened by the clear air and the strong sunlight, give a character to the scenery unlike anything else to be found.

Travelers all notice also that this is a very silent land. The want of moisture and the absence of verdure are attended by a consequent absence of life. No tinkling rivulets, no hum of insects, no roar of business or rush of travel, vibrate on the air. With us such sounds, unnoticed, are falling continually on the ear, giving unconsciously a perpetual feeling of society. There all is hushed, and everything is silent as the place of death and the grave.

* Palmer's Exodus, page 217.   † Bonar's Sinai.

The result is, that when a passing traveler speaks, his voice has an unwonted effect. Everything is distinctly heard. All the ordinary conversation of a party passing at a distance comes ringing clear upon the air. A book read aloud at the top of a great mountain is heard at the base. A little sandslide, starting from some summit, gives a metallic echo and tinkles like a bell. And when on some rare occasion a storm breaks across the desert, the majestic thunder-voice is caught up and tossed from one headland to another, till at last it rolls away down the wadys and dies out upon the sea. The echoes in some parts are wonderful.* Every sound is taken up and repeated by a hundred airy tongues. The monks of the convent of St. Catharine are said to have been frightened off from the original location of their abode on Mt. Moses by strange noises, and had in consequence to establish themselves on a lower level. The little sandslides gave them an impression of a convent bell ringing inside the mountain.†

In the recent work of E. H. Palmer, M. A., on the Exodus, we have a curious account of these desert sounds, particularly at Jebel Nagus. Nagus signifies a wooden gong, such as is used

---

* Bonar, Sinai, page 115.   † Sinai and Palestine, page 15.

instead of a bell in Eastern churches, and the mountain receives its name from the gong-like noises heard at times in the vicinity. It is a height composed of friable sandstone, of a white color; and on a slope toward the south-west is a bed of drift-sand reaching to an altitude of three hundred and eighty feet. This bed lies at an angle of about thirty degrees to the horizon, and is so fine and dry as to be easily set in motion. When this occurs, the sand rolls down with a sluggish sticky motion, and the sound begins—at first a low vibratory moan, but gradually swelling into a roar like thunder, then as gradually dying away. The sounds are louder where the surface is heated by the sun, and a change of temperature, a gust of wind or the accident of a gazelle running across the bed sets the sand in motion. The Arabs declare that the sounds are only heard on Fridays and Sundays, and have a very strange legend as to their origin.*

How strangely such scenery and such peculiarities must have affected the children of Israel one can well imagine. From the flat lands of Goshen to the tumultuous wildness of those awful heights was as great a change as could be well conceived. What sentiments of sublimity would

* Palmer's Exodus, page 181.

rise in their minds while passing under the shadow of those granite pinnacles! How they would listen to those echoes, wakened each day by the trumpet call to break camp! The very desolation of the country would bring its influence unconsciously over them, and they could scarcely look up without feeling that He who created the world was a great and terrible God.

They did not reach the more rugged part of the peninsula, however, on first crossing the sea. They came to it by gradual approach. Their place of encampment after the "night to be remembered" was upon a broad gravelly plain (Ex. xv. 22), beyond which rose the great wall of limestone rock known as the er-Rahah mountains. This range was a mountain only on the side toward them. From its summit extends an immense plateau called the Desert of Tih, or desert of the wanderings. Across this plateau there is a little strip of sand-desert, almost the only thing of the kind found on the peninsula.* It lies at the foot of those great sandstone mountains which form the outworks of Sinai. Where the children of Israel traveled there was no difficulty with sand; and it is one of the con-

* Robinson's Researches, I., 111.

firmations of Scripture to which no small weight is to be attached that, while we have a very minute account of their troubles by the way, such a thing as a sand-storm or a sand-path is never once mentioned. They were in a desert, but not a desert of sand. Their path was at first over a hard gravelly plain, and afterward, till they reached Mount Sinai, mostly up a wide wady that looked like "a way prepared for the ransomed of the Lord to pass over."

XXV.

THE FIRST DESERT TROUBLE, THIRST.

IT is not likely that the camp would move immediately after the crossing of the sea. They had passed a very exciting night, and needed a little time for calmer thought. They were wearied with their journey, and had need of rest. Some arrangements of great importance also needed to be made for their passage through the desert. They must carry at least a partial supply of food and water. They were sadly in need of more tents; and as they had now no enemy to fear, they could wait and put everything in readiness before they moved.

While they were thus resting in camp, it was proposed to have a celebration. A whole nation emancipated, and especially a people delivered as they had been by the passage of the Red Sea, might indulge in some rejoicing. Nay, they owed it to God who had delivered them to set apart a day in which to unite in some expression of gratitude to his name. So they made ready, and Moses wrote a hymn for them to sing on the occasion, and they practiced upon the music till they could sing it responsively; and when the day came everything went off with great eclat.

Among the services of that remarkable occasion was some performance which they called dancing; and as this is one of the incidents sometimes urged in defence of the dance of modern society, it is well, perhaps, to see what it was. In the first place, then, it was a religious service, and not mere amusement; in the next place, it was a dance in which the women engaged, but in which the men did not mingle with them; in the next place, they so danced as to sing and play the timbrel while dancing; and last of all, it was such a dance that they were led in it by Miriam, Moses' sister, who was now a woman above eighty years old. When the dance of modern society answers to this description, and is held in the open air and by daylight, it will be liable to very little objection.

This religious service probably closed their stay at that place, and the next morning, with the first glimpse of daylight, the camp was astir and the people were preparing for the march. Their water-skins were filled from the wells hard by; such provisions as could most easily be obtained were hastily packed up. The cattle were driven in from the valleys where they had been pasturing. The pillar of cloud was uplifted, and the train moved on.

The line of march is toward Mount Sinai. Indeed, from the start it has been rather in that direction than toward Palestine. They have an errand there. So on they go, fresh and free, now beguiling their way with songs, now listening to the ripple of the waves along the seashore, and often fanned by the breeze that comes in fresh from the cool water. Some of the time they are out upon a hard gravelly plain. Sometimes deep gullies cross their track. Sometimes they pass over little eminences where they have an extensive view of the country. Sometimes they pass in behind the hills that hug the shore, losing sight of the sea for an hour, and then they crowd the beach again, crushing the white shells at every footfall.

A good day's march would be about ten miles. At the close of the first day all was well. They went into camp, slept soundly and awoke fresh for another day's work. The desert air is always invigorating except in the extreme heat of the day, and they felt new vigor as they rose to begin again. Then the clear sunshine put everything in cheerful aspect, and the novelty of the scene occupied their attention. So a second day closed and all was still well.

Then a third morning dawned, and with good hope they once more addressed themselves to their journey. They were beginning to be a little wearied, however, by this time; and though they were ashamed to complain, they marched more silently, and were quite ready to be discouraged if any misfortune should occur. Toward noon the misfortune came. The news of it soon spread through the camp, and the consternation was very great—their supply of water was exhausted.

"How far might it be to some stream?" The question brought a grim smile over their hard faces. A stream in that country would probably be very interesting when any one should find it.

"Was there not a spring, then, or a well, or at least some sort of pool where the rains collected?" No answer; there was no sign of it.

So hot noon was upon them; and the children, always thirsty when there is no means of giving them drink, were crying; and the faces of the people were flushed; and the dust raised by their million feet was breathed in and lodged in their dry throats; and their tongues began to be parched and their eyes swollen; and at last some were found fainting by the way. The leaders urged them on, however; and as there was nothing else for them, they did their best to continue the journey, when, just as the last hope was disappearing, they were startled by a cry of joy. It came from the front. "Water! water!" went up the shout, and in a few moments all could see it for themselves—that is, all could see a growth of green bushes just before them, and they knew that where those bushes were water was sure to be found.

They hurried up, and sure enough they found it. It was abundant, apparently pure, certainly clear and cool, and they eagerly knelt along the margin to quaff the crystal treasure. But what is this? They turn suddenly away scowling. The water is bitter; they might as well have drank from the sea. Do not wonder if they murmured. It was a terrible trial, but God sent them deliverance in a way all his own. Moses was directed to cast a certain "tree" into the water, which he did, and its bitterness quite disappeared.

This was their first great desert trouble, thirst. They called the place Marah—bitterness. It is supposed to be the same as the modern fountain Howarah, and it helps to understand the story to know that, while the quality of this water is not in general good, it varies considerably at different times. Mr. Palmer,* in his recent explorations in that country, found it "not only drinkable, but palatable," and it is not at all improbable that Moses had found it good both on his flight out of Egypt and on his return. When the fountain is quite full, it is very good, but as it dries away the proportion of saline matter becomes greater, till it is nearly worthless. The children of Israel probably arrived there at a time when it was partly dried away.

Near this fountain grows a bush, supposed to be the same with which Moses healed the water; and as the bush bears an acid juicy berry which improves the taste of the brackish desert springs,

* Palmer's Exodus, page 45.

some have supposed that the people merely crushed this berry into their cups before drinking. But the berries are never so abundant as to sweeten the water for two million people, and this adventure also occurred at a season when the berries would be unfit for use. They reached this fountain some time in April. The berries do not ripen before June.*

A still more satisfactory relief from this desert trouble was obtained a little farther on. They probably encamped at Marah for the night, but there was was a better place for encamping at the end of the next day's journey. That was Elim, where there were "twelve fountains of water and threescore and ten palm trees." These are the outlines of a picture which one easily fills up.

There is a little difference of opinion in regard to the exact locality of Elim. Two small valleys cross their track at the distance of about a day's march from Howarah, Wady Ghurundel and Wady Useit. Mr. Stanley thinks that, if we judge by the number of palm trees, Elim must be the same as Wady Useit. But Dr. Bonar, who was at the pains to count the trees at both places, says they are far more numerous at Wady

---

* Robinson's Researches, I., page 98, 139.

Ghurundel, and it is there that most travelers have located Elim.*

Wady Ghurundel is not only a valley of palm trees, but of tamarisk and acacia, making quite a little forest;† and when the children of Israel encamped there, they found a brook flowing down the glen.‡ Wells could also be dug with very little trouble, and the place was the most desirable they had seen since they came out of Egypt.

So there they rested a while. The cattle easily found forage in the surrounding wadys. What tents they had were pitched along the brookside, and others were rapidly preparing. The palms extended a welcome shade over their heads, the birds were singing among the branches, and the gurgle of that brook—ah! that, for a desert sound, was sweeter than all.

Human life, like the desert, has its green places. After peculiar hardships God sometimes sends us peculiar favors. We come to Marah and are disappointed, but Elim lies just beyond.

* Palmer's Exodus, page 46.
† Bonar's Sinai, page 122, 124.
‡ Robinson's Researches, I., page 199.

XXVI.

A NEW TROUBLE, HUNGER.

THE Israelites were about six weeks journeying from Egypt to Mount Sinai, so we know that nearly four weeks were spent in resting by the way. Two weeks of steady travel, even at the rate they moved, should have sufficed for the entire journey. One of their chief resting-places we naturally locate at Elim. Why should they leave that delightful spot? It is not likely that they stayed there less than a week. It might have been twice as long.

At last, however, the signal came that they must prepare once more to march. They must start early, too, for this day they must make a journey of nearly sixteen miles. This they could well afford to do after so delightful a rest.

By sunrise, then, behold them moving once more. They are coming into the mountain region now, and they begin to find an uneven way. Ascending the ridge that divides Ghurundel from Useit, they see yet on their left the great rocky wall of the er-Rahah, only its name changes here to Tih.* Close in the advance, on

---
* See Map at Chapter XXII.

the right, rises a very different eminence, known as Mount Humman. Straight before them, but much farther on, shooting up from a wilderness of lesser summits, is Mount Serbal, the first of those bare granitic mountains they have yet seen, which make the core of this strange land.

Down from this ridge they pass into Wady Useit. It is Elim on a smaller scale. Then they go over a second ridge and descend into Wady Thal. A third ridge is crossed, and they are in Wady Shubeikeh. This valley they follow a short distance, as it bears in the direction they wished to go, and then pass out of it into Wady Taiyibeh, which they follow four miles farther, when it brings them out again to the sea.

Here they encamp. Num. xxxiii. 10. Probably the darkness of night is fully upon them, and certainly they are sufficiently weary to sleep soundly. It has been the hardest day's work they have had since coming out of Egypt. But it is worth something to have a sight again of the familiar sea; and the breeze comes up fresh from the water, and the stars keep sentry in the sky, and they dream, perhaps, of the green fields of Goshen and the delicious waters of the Nile.

Here we encounter uncertainty. In what

direction did they next move? Toward Mount Sinai, of course. But by which of two routes? If they chose to do so, they could move still southward along a narrow strip of sand that fringes the shore, coming out upon the plain El Markha, which in that case would be the wilderness of Sin. But, if they preferred, they could retrace their steps up Wady Taiyibeh, and by a succession of mountain-passes make their way to Wady Feiran. Many travelers have regarded this second route as the more probable, but Mr. Palmer,* whose recent surveys in that country excel all others in accuracy, is strongly inclined to the former supposition. It is not likely they would come down to the seashore only to retrace their steps up the wady; and it is not at all improbable that, at the very time of the exodus, at least a small force of Egyptian soldiers would have been encountered on the interior route. Copper-mining was extensively carried on at that time in these wadys, and there was always a military guard set over the workmen.†

El Markha is described as a very monotonous and gloomy place, shut in against the sea by a long range of white chalk hills, without pasturage, without water, without life. The Arabs

* Palmer's Exodus, page 196. † Ibid., page 194.

never came to the spot except to hasten across it on their way to and from Suez.

Just in this gloomy place the Israelites encounter famine. Their meal-bags have been growing light for some days; now the last one has been shaken out, and there is not another mouthful in the whole camp. Their provisions are gone and their faces are still desertward. There is no relief before them, so far as they can see. They have already been nearly a month out of Egypt, and the wonder is that their supply had lasted so long.

When a man suffers by himself alone, he can endure it, but these men have their families with them. Their little children are crying for bread, and at every step they are plunging deeper into that great and terrible desert from which they cannot hope for any supply. "And the whole congregation murmured against Moses and against Aaron."

It was not so strange that they murmured, perhaps, but those people could never groan without cursing. So, as they dared not say anything directly against God, they took the men who stood nearest God and vented their displeasure on them. They sat down and talked about the good things they used to have in

Egypt, as if their lot had been the happiest there that ever men enjoyed. They wished they had died there rather than come to such an awful place. They did not believe that Moses had any good motive in bringing them there. He meant to kill them, they believed, and perhaps seize on their property. So they talked.

It was all very unreasonable, no doubt, but famine is a hard subject to hold an argument with. It was very wicked in them also, no doubt, but certainly we must admit that they were sorely tried. At any rate, when God does not condemn, it ill becomes men with like infirmities to speak harshly of the conduct of their brethren.

All these murmurings on the way to Mount Sinai were overcome by love. All such murmurings after their leaving Mount Sinai were severely punished. Now they were just entering upon a new course of life, and must not be discouraged; now they knew not God, and were ignorant of his laws, and must not be held to a very strict reckoning. At Mount Sinai they were about to receive instruction, and after that the case would be different. There they would come under a well-defined law, and that law must not be broken. He that knoweth the will of his Master, and doeth it not, shall be beaten with many stripes.

In the present case, therefore, they are only reminded that God understands the nature of those murmurings, and that they have not deceived him at all by using Moses' name in the case, and then a promise is given that relief shall be forthcoming. That relief was to be twofold. Part of it would come that very evening, and the remainder the next day.

About sunset, therefore, what should they see but a great flock of birds flying toward the camp? They flew very low, and the people began catching them; and when they were caught, behold, they were quails, as delicious a morsel for eating as a man could ask for. Such flocks of quails often light upon the desert in spring-time, wearied with their long flight across the sea. About a year later these people encountered just such another flock on the opposite side of the peninsula, near the Gulf of Akabah. Num. xi. 31. In that case the blessing brought an awful curse with it. In this, however, the people took no harm. They all ate till they were satisfied, and then lay down to rest, curious to know what was to come in the morning.

Probably there were some early risers in the camp the next day. Indeed, in the desert early rising is common. The pure air gives vigor to the system, and the bright sunlight of early morning puts sleep to flight. On this morning there were people out long before the shadows were dispersed, and as the light increased they saw something on the ground about them that attracted their attention. It looked like frost, they said, using the best comparison they could think of. We should perhaps have thought it a light fall of snow. It seemed to be left there by the dew, and the plain was quite white with it. "Man-hu?" they said one to another in the Hebrew tongue—"Man-hu?"—what is it? And the word "Man-hu?" flies about the camp till it gets to be the name by which this curious thing is known. Moses told them what it was, but they never would call it anything else; it was always man-hu, or, as we have it, manna.

It was in kernels, like grains of rice; and they scraped it up from the sand and the rocks and immediately began to use it. They ground it in mills, baked it, boiled it and used it in every way like a grain. Num. xi. 6. The taste, in one form, was like wafers made of honey. Ex. xvi. 31. Prepared in a different way, it still more perfectly suited the Oriental appetite, for it was like fresh oil. Num. xi. 8.

Some have tried to identify this manna with a species of honey-dew that drips from the tamarisk. Such honey-dew is called manna, but it differs from this sent to the children of Israel in almost every particular. Honey-dew is medicinal; this was for daily food: honey-dew is not capable of being ground in mills or baked or boiled; honey-dew never comes in quantities sufficient for such a multitude, even if it were a wholesome food; and honey-dew never falls, as that did, in double quantities on the day before the Sabbath and on a plain where the tamarisk does not grow. The simplest view of this narrative is the best. God sent the manna by miracle, and nothing of the kind was ever seen before or afterward. It was, in some respects, the greatest of all the miracles, for it continued without interruption forty years.

At the giving of the manna special notice is taken of the Sabbath. This is the first clear and distinct mention of that day after its original institution. True, we have some intimations of a division of time by weeks, but who among mankind, from Adam to Moses, kept the Sabbath day? Did Noah? We cannot tell. Did Abraham or Isaac or Jacob? No one can answer. Did the children of Israel in Egypt? It is not very likely; their taskmasters gave them few holidays.

But with the manna God takes occasion to resuscitate the old institution. To-morrow is the Sabbath (Ex. xvi. 23), says Moses. He does not tell them that it shall be a Sabbath; he merely indicates the day. He does not direct them to set apart a day as a new thing; he only tells them what day has been set apart for them from the ancient times. So, as they had their first religious festival at the Red Sea, they have now their first Sabbath at the wilderness of Sin.

The word Sin, in this connection, has no reference to their transgression there; it is a Hebrew term having the same root as Sinai. This wilderness of Sin was simply the wilderness of Seneh or Sinai, so named from its neighborhood, the Sinai country.

XXVII.

THE NEXT STAGE, THIRST AGAIN.

THE seventeenth chapter of Exodus conveys us by a single sentence from the wilderness of Sin to Rephidim, but the more detailed history in the thirty-third chapter of Numbers mentions two stopping-places by the way. These are Dophkah and Alush, stations somewhere in what is now called Wady Feiran, but which was anciently called Pharan or Paran. They reached this valley a little beyond El Markha, and very soon were again among the palms, the springs and the brooks of running water. A sudden turn in the road brings the scene unexpectedly before them. The cliffs on either hand again towered above them, as in Taiyibeh, perpendicular and bare, but the valley was carpeted with green.* Even to this day a dense grove extends for miles up the valley, and the traveler finds himself all at once passing into the unpruned wilderness of a tropical luxuriance. He has reached an oasis, and one that was evidently still more extensive and luxuriant in the ancient times. It was another Elim, only on a larger scale. After a great trouble a great mercy indeed.

They cannot stay in this happy valley, however. They are on a pilgrimage, and time is passing. So they soon break camp again and are once more on the move. Now their way is

* Life Scenes, page 344.

rugged; the path becomes steeper — almost a stairway — but still they climb on. At last, after many turns and much toil, they reach the heights, and the way is comparatively easy. On their left a broad wady opens to the east. Before them, from the south, a circuitous gorge, known in modern times as the Wady es Sheikh, comes down from Mount Sinai, the summit of that mountain being not more than about ten miles away. And here they halt, overwearied with their late journeyings and once more entirely without water.

It is here that Mr. Holland, who accompanied Mr. Palmer's party, places Rephidim,* not in Wady Feiran, but in Wady es Sheikh; and though he stood alone in this view, the remainder of the party dissenting, it certainly agrees well with the inspired narrative.

It was no mere inconvenience they were brought to when they were without water, nor was it a mere question of severe suffering; it would soon be a matter of life and death with them. Unless they could be supplied with water, and that very soon, the whole caravan would perish.

In their distress, therefore, as was natural,

* Palmer's Exodus, page 228.

they went to Moses, but it was the old story—out of temper as soon as in trouble, and never knowing how to ask for help without doing something to show that they did not deserve any favor. They had been kindly delivered at Marah. Why not ask in a humble way for the same deliverance here? Moses was indeed their leader, but was not he himself led by the pillar of cloud and of fire? He was not responsible for their pilotage, neither had he ever promised to supply them with drink by the way. But they assail him with violent demonstrations, and seem inclined to deal with him more rudely than ever before. "And Moses cried unto the Lord, and said, What shall I do unto this people? they be almost ready to stone me." Ex. xvii. 4. We know not precisely what form the uprising took on that occasion, but it was something that made a deep impression on Moses: "He called the place Massah and Meribah because of the chiding of the children of Israel, and because they tempted the Lord, saying, Is the Lord among us or not?" All that in sight of the pillar of cloud!—all that, after such a history!—strife and temptation! Massah and Meribah! Truly, one would by this time have expected something better.

Rather shall we not say that one would have

expected something worse?—some mark of God's displeasure as a suitable testimony against this repeated provocation—some judgment stroke to fall upon at least the guilty leaders of this revolt? But he met them in mercy once more.

He told Moses to take the elders of Israel, or chiefs of the tribes, up with him to Horeb, saying that they would see him there "standing upon a rock." This meant that they should see the pillar of cloud in that position. When the rock was thus indicated, he added, Moses must smite it with the rod in his hand, on which it was promised that the waters should gush out in sufficient quantities to supply the multitude.

So Moses made haste and departed. The distance was such that he would reach the place not far from sunset. When he arrived at the spot, there indeed was the rock, and there the pillar of cloud resting on it. The chieftains gathered around, and Moses stood in the midst of them. The rod was uplifted and the blow was struck, and following quick upon the blow there was a great rent in the rock, and out gushed the waters. It was no mere trickling stream—it was a great brook, almost a river; and it rapidly poured down the wady toward the camp. The people must have retired to rest before the waters reached them, but it would be an uneasy rest, thirsting as they were, and no sound would more quickly awaken them than the sound of flowing water. It came rushing down the slope, gurgling among the stones, chafing against the rocks, roaring in cascades and filling the night air with a strange tumult. Some one heard it and shouted, "Water!" and his call was answered in another part of the camp by the cry of "Water!" and there was the lowing of cattle and the bleating of sheep, as the thirsty creatures snuffed the air, and all the camp was soon astir echoing the glad cry, "Water, water!" In a moment it was running right past their tent doors, and man and beast, side by side, bowed their head to the passing current, and drank and were satisfied.

Travelers find a rock in this region which from its position and peculiarities might be the one that was smitten by Moses. It has several horizontal fissures, evidently water worn, and a number of persons, who have been skeptical on the subject before seeing it, have been convinced by visiting the spot that this was indeed the rock of this story.* Others do not yield to this opinion, but none deny that such a remarkable rock

---

* Kitto, Script. Read.

exists in the vicinity of Horeb. The water flowing from this rock would naturally reach the sea by the eastern slope, in the general direction the children of Israel were to travel when they should leave Mount Sinai. And it was this stream, keeping them company, which perhaps occasioned the apostle's expression, "For they drank of that spiritual Rock *which followed them;* and that Rock was Christ." 1 Cor. x. 4.

The two great wants of the mighty host are, therefore, permanently supplied at last. For food, they have the daily supply of manna; for drink, they have this water fresh from the rock; and they wait in camp till further orders shall come to go forward. While they are waiting one or two adventures occur which need to be related.

XXVIII.

WAR.

THE country through which the Israelites had been passing, though called a desert, was not entirely uninhabited. Its more favored portions, like Wady Feiran, sustained quite a population, and it was just beyond this region of upland, upon the borders of which they were now encamped, where Moses met Raguel when he first fled out of Egypt.

The principal tribe of this region were the Amalekites, who traced their descent from Amalek, the grandson of Esau. Gen. xxxvi. 12. They were a somewhat powerful people, being scattered over the country on the north of the Sinaitic peninsula, quite up to the borders of Palestine. Indeed, they were apparently so powerful that some have doubted whether their ancestry must not be traced to a remoter date than we have given. Nor were they entirely a roving people, dwelling in tents, for remains of their houses can to this day be traced in Wady Feiran.*

They occupied this Sinaitic peninsula by ancient right; and when they saw the vast hordes of Israelites invading their territory and encamping in their fairest oases, they doubted what it should mean. Besides this, they were a plundering people, and the flocks and the herds which were driven along with the moving caravan, and that Egyptian jewelry which the Israelites displayed, presented a tempting prize. They could not bring forward any military force sufficient to

* Kitto, Script. Read.

match that of the Israelites, but they could hang upon their rear, hover about their flanks, and occasionally dash boldly into some unguarded part of the camp and come off with rich booty. It was a daring business on their part, especially as they could see the pillar of cloud continually, but they "feared not God" (Deut. xxv. 8), and the temptation was too strong to be resisted.

For a long time they contented themselves with these more or less successful raids; but as the Israelites pushed farther into the interior, they gathered in greater numbers and became more bold, till, at last, taking possession of a narrow pass through which the Israelites were about to march, they drew up in battle array, and disputed their farther passage. Nothing was left, therefore, for Moses but to take up the gage of battle. Arrangements were accordingly made, and a force was sent forward to clear the pass.

In this trial the children of Israel behaved themselves handsomely. There was no cowardly outcry, as when they saw Pharaoh's chariots, nor any quarreling with Moses, nor any murmuring against God. They had been so vexed and perplexed by these Amalekites that, when at last they had an opportunity to give them battle, they seem rather to have hailed it with pleasure.

Moses, probably more than any one else, saw the difficulties of the case. The Israelites were encumbered with their families, and at best but poorly armed. They had never been in battle, either, and it was quite a question whether they would not run at the first onset of the Amalekites. But calling out a young man named Joshua, and putting him in command, Moses took Aaron his brother, and Hur his brother-in-law, and climbed a hill from which he could watch the contest, and where he could give himself to prayer.

Joshua led the troops gallantly forward to the attack, and Moses lifted up the rod by which he had wrought such wonders hitherto. While the rod was held aloft, Joshua pressed the Amalekites backward; when the rod was lowered, the Amalekites in turn crowded back the army of Israel. And as Moses' hands grew weary and he was unable to hold the rod on high continually, the day went on with changing fortunes. At last Aaron and Hur came to the rescue, and on each side of him stayed up his hands, when the Amalekites began to give way on every side, and were completely defeated.

It was a good thing that Moses had help that day, and it was a great thing for the people that they won that battle. It ended their troubles with the Amalekites, and it gave them courage for any encounters they might have with other enemies by the way. The impiety of the Amalekites on this occasion, in attacking a people so manifestly under the protection of God, is strongly marked in the Scripture story. Moses was ordered to write it in a book and leave it in charge of the generations to come after, that Israel should never cease to make war on that heaven-daring people until they were exterminated. Saul (1 Sam. xv. 9), in later years, undertook to disregard this command in the case of King Agag, and it cost him his throne. The last of these Amalekites of whom we have any account was Haman (Esth. vii. 10), probably a descendant of Agag, and with him and his sons perished the accursed race.

We all have our battle-days, but the fiercest fight in which the Christian engages is when he fights against his own indwelling sin. In all such conflicts it is a good thing to have human helpers. The Aarons and the Hurs who stay up our hands help us more than they sometimes are aware of. Still, all our sufficiency is of God. He may send deliverance through the channel of ordinary cause and effect, but none the less it comes from his hand. When Moses reared a monument on that battle-field, it was not one inscribed with his own name, nor yet with the name of the brave young general who commanded—the victory was the Lord's, and to him was ascribed the glory. His memorial monument was an altar, around which they worshiped God, and on that altar he put the inscription, "The Lord my banner," and pledged himself to carry into execution the awful charge to exterminate Amalek from off the earth.

Soon after this battle it is announced to Moses that a company of visitors have arrived at the camp desirous of an interview with him. On going out to meet them he finds there his wife and his two sons, whom Jethro, his brother-in-law, has brought out to meet him. Moses details somewhat to Jethro the Lord's dealings with him, and recites to him his manner of governing the people. Jethro takes the liberty to suggest that his administration might be improved upon. Moses is burdening himself with too many cares. He needs a class of subordinate officers to assist him. Let the people make the choice, but let there be a class of new rulers appointed—rulers over hundreds, rulers over fifties, and rulers over tens—and let Moses' strength be reserved for those weightier matters in which the wisdom of his subordinates fails.

Moses was pleased with this advice and adopted the arrangement. And Jethro rejoiced in all the goodness God had shown to his people, and united with Moses in an act of solemn worship. Ex. xviii. 12. And this friendship between the family of Jethro and the children of Israel is seen generations afterward. 1 Sam. xv. 6.

XXIX.

THE MOUNT OF GOD.

IN making our way to Mount Sinai we have passed what some have regarded as that spot, and perhaps it is due to an ancient tradition to go back and examine those claims.

Coming up the Wady Feiran, about a good day's march below Rephidim, there is seen upon the right one of the finest mountain-summits of all this region. It stands at a distance of about three miles from the wady, and is reached by a deep rocky gorge. Its height is between six and seven thousand feet above the sea-level, and its top terminates in half a dozen sharp conical peaks. There are greater heights farther

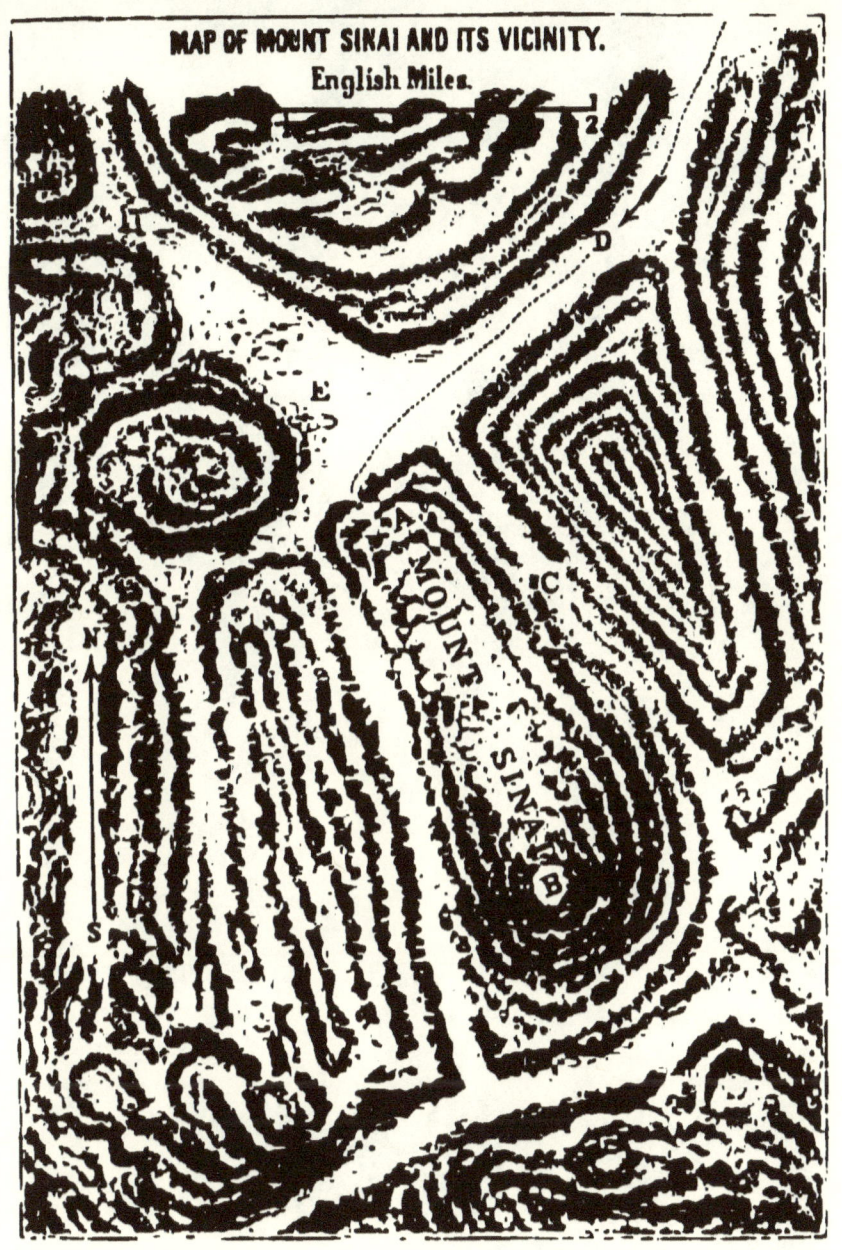

on, but they rise from higher surroundings, and therefore do not stand out so boldly. This one is a sort of corner tower of the central granitic region, and lifting its summit from a lower level, secures a grandeur of appearance which can be claimed for no other mountain on the Sinaitic peninsula. This is Mount Serbal.* Lepsius held it to be the true Sinai. The ancient traditions also strongly favor the idea, and the Arabs from remotest memory have always attached to it associations of great sacredness. It is a majestic summit, worthy to have been the scene of the giving of the law, but it does not afford the requisite conditions of that event as recorded in Scripture. When the law was given, the children of Israel encamped so close against the mount "where God was" that bounds had to be set to prevent their crowding up against it; but there is no camping-ground at the base of Mount Serbal, nor at any place nearer than Wady Feiran, three miles away.

We have passed on, therefore, in our journeyings, beyond Mount Serbal, following the circuitous track of the Wady es Sheikh, and have found Rephidim at a point where another wady breaks over the watershed therefrom, opening a

* Sinai and Palestine, page 39.

highway down toward the east. The water from the smitten rock at Horeb has come in a swift stream down to the junction of these wadys and is flowing off in the easterly direction, and we are to follow the brook upward from Rephidim to its source.

The great caravan, therefore, is moving again. Its course lies toward the south-west, along a narrow valley, for eight or ten miles, when it comes out upon an open plain. Abutting upon that plain on its south-eastern edge are three mountain-heads, and the central one of the three is Mount Sinai. It has not the grandeur of the solitary Serbal, but it is, nevertheless, a majestic summit, and the plain at its base supplies all the conditions of the sacred narrative.* This summit is called by the Arabs Ras Sasefeh.† It is the termination of a rugged range about three miles long, running in a south-easterly direction. The opposite termination of the same range is called Mount Moses (Jebel Mousa), and the whole range, taken together, is called Horeb or Sinai— terms also frequently used to embrace the surrounding country.

As the children of Israel marched in upon this plain from the north-east, this mountain

---

* Rob. Res., I., page 140.   † Stanley, Sin. and Pal., page 42.

rose almost directly before them, towering above all the other summits of that neighborhood. It was a bare black rock, shooting sheer up from the level ground to the height of fourteen hundred feet, and presenting a surface broad,

MOUNT SINAI.

massive, and broken into gloomy recesses and jagged hollows. The plain spreads out at its foot to the breadth of about two miles in its widest direction,* measuring perhaps one-third

* Robinson's Researches, I.

of a mile in the opposite way. This, however, does not include the entire camping capacity of the place, for various wadys and recesses open into the plain, from which, for a considerable distance, the mountain is plainly visible.

Here, then, they stand at the end of the first great stage in their pilgrimage. They had reached the Mount of God, and to mark the date exactly we have it: "In the third month, when the children of Israel were gone forth out of the land of Egypt, the same day came they into the wilderness of Sinai; and there Israel camped before the mount." Ex. xix. 1, 2. If this third month meant the third new moon, as Professor Bush suggests, the time out would now be forty-five days, making the season about the first of June. The year is reckoned about 1491 B. C.

They had been led through many dangers, but out of them all the Lord had delivered them. They had gone up into the very heart of a desert country, but he had supplied them with food and drink. They had sometimes behaved themselves very wickedly, but the Lord had forgiven them. And now, as they looked back over that marvelous history—the plagues, the Red Sea and the desert—to that hour, how must their hearts have swelled with wonder, with gratitude and with joy!

They had been brought there to meet their God. On that black and awful summit before them even now he has set the pillar of cloud; and around the plain on every hand rise those desolate pinnacles which seem to shut them in from all the world. They are there, remote from all the usual haunts of men, waiting in silence to hear what God will say.

XXX.

THE GIVING OF THE LAW.

THE camp was no sooner quiet than Moses received intimation that he was wanted up in the mountain where God was, and on going up he received a message with which he was to return to the people. This began his going to and fro between God and the children of Israel. He was their mediator, carrying messages from God to the people and returning with the people's answer to God. In this office he was a type of Christ.

The message which he first brought down to the people was in these words: "Ye have seen what I did unto the Egyptians, and how I bare you on eagles' wings, and brought you unto myself. Now therefore, if ye will obey my voice indeed, and keep my covenant, then ye shall be a peculiar treasure unto me above all people: for all the earth is mine: and ye shall be unto me a kingdom of priests, and a holy nation." Ex. xix. 4, 5.

The purport of this message was that they should choose for themselves, after what they had seen, whether they would accept this peculiar relation to God or not. He had shown by his mercies what great love he had for them, and how well able he was to defend them. Would they like such a Being now for their King? If so, he will regard them as a precious treasure; and through them, as a priestly nation, he will communicate with the people of the whole world. What have they to say? Will they accept the offer and obey his voice?

Their answer was very prompt; and considering their recent rebellion, it might have been considered a little hasty, perhaps, but no doubt it came from the heart: "And the people answered together, and said, All that the Lord hath spoken we will do. And Moses returned the words of the people unto the Lord." Ex. xix. 8. They had elected Jehovah their national God and King. This election was subsequently ratified by a certain solemnity which they observed, but it was here that the choice was made. The Lord Jehovah should be their God and King.

When Moses returned with this answer, God announced to him that he would now speak to the people. They would see him coming down in a thick cloud upon the top of the mountain, and they should hear his voice, every man for himself. The reason assigned for this was "that they may believe thee for ever." Unless they should hear God for themselves, they might some time raise the question whether Moses were not deceiving them. "Who knows?" they would say. "Has the Lord spoken or not? We have Moses' word for it, and that is all."

God intended to shut off all such caviling. He would so utter his voice that no one should ever question it. He would come down upon the mountain, in sight of the whole camp, and they should all hear what he had to say.

Moses carried this announcement to the people and ordered them to make suitable preparation for the august occasion. He set the time—on the third day. Then God was coming down, and he would appear in great state. The people must make haste to wash their travel-stained garments and appear in clean attire. There must be a boundary marked also along the base of the mountain, beyond which no man must pass, on pain of death. If even one of their cattle inadvertently passed that line, it must be immediately stoned or thrust through with a dart. When the King came, they would hear a trumpet sounding before him; and at that signal they must all come out from their tents and gather in a great congregation to receive him. But let them be very careful not to cross the prescribed bounds.

So they hastened their preparations, and the great day dawned. It was ushered in with an awful thunder-peal, one gun at daybreak startling the still sleeping camp and sending its echoes down the long defiles.

The people hastened to their tent doors, and of course the first glance of every eye was toward the mountain. There it stood, beneath the gray morning sky, and upon its summit the pillar of cloud, now a heavy, darkened mass, as if charged with other thunders or with coming rain. Every moment the air grew darker. The sun, that had just risen and cast its bright light over the scene, was obscured. The whole heaven grew black, and a mysterious twilight fell upon the plain. Then there came another thunder-peal. How it shook the earth! and how the mountain-peaks around took up the echo, and sent it across that silent land till it died away upon the distant sea! Then more thunders, and with them vivid lightnings—broad flashes glaring across the dim desolations round. Whole parks of celestial artillery were exploding, stunning the ear with their loud detonations. And in the midst of all and above all, at last, the expected trumpet sound. God had come: the people must come out to meet him.

They pressed forward and stood in a vast semicircle around the mountain, filling the plain in every direction. Still the thunders crash, the lightnings leap from the bosom of the dark cloud and the trumpet sounds louder and louder. Then two additional phenomena are introduced which still heighten the scene. First there is an earthquake, rocking the solid ground beneath their feet and heaving old Sinai to and fro as if it were about to be hurled down. Then a fire bursts from the mountain—not the lightning, but red flames roaring round the pinnacles, and dense masses of smoke rolling up the summit and mingling with the cloud that rests there.

Just as the scene had reached this height,

"Moses spake, and God answered by a voice." What Moses said is not here recorded, but the apostle Paul, in giving the history of this occasion, says, "And so terrible was the sight that even Moses said, I do exceedingly fear and quake." Heb. xii. 21. And if Moses used any such language, this was exactly the place for it.

God's answer, "by a voice," was to the effect that he should come up into the mount. This was a remarkable direction to be given to one who was so greatly terrified already; but Moses obeyed, and received from God the charge to go immediately back again and tell the people once more "not to break through the bounds unto the Lord to gaze." Ex. xx. 21.

This charge was especially intended for the priests, so called; for though no divinely-appointed priesthood existed yet among them, by common law all their tribal chieftains exercised that sacred function. Perhaps there was some movement among these priests looking toward what had been forbidden. Perhaps they supposed the bounds that were set about the mount were intended to restrain the common people only, and certainly it was very much like them to peer into those awful mysteries, and, if possible, gaze upon the hidden God.

At any rate, Moses hastened down with the order; and as the priests fell back to their places, the thunder and the trumpet ceased, and there was a great silence. Then came the Voice, saying, "I am the Lord thy God, which have brought thee out of the land of Egypt, out of the house of bondage." Then followed the ten commandments, after which all the scene was renewed, with even additional terrors. "And all the people saw the thunderings and the lightnings, and the noise of the trumpet, and the mountain smoking: and when the people saw it, they removed and stood afar off."

It was the first and last time that God spoke to them without a mediator. They could not endure it. "And they said unto Moses, Speak thou with us and we will hear, but let not God speak with us, lest we die." Ex. xx. 19.

This remarkable theophany must have produced a profound impression. No one who had witnessed the wonders of that day could easily forget. Even at this distance of time and with these imperfect ideas of the occasion, we recognize in it something unspeakably grand.

XXXI.

IN THE MOUNT.

ONE circumstance attending the giving of the law is singularly omitted in the Mosaic narrative. Nothing is said of the angels that appeared on the occasion, and it is only by gathering up certain fragmentary expressions from the later books of Scripture that we know that any such thing occurred. In the great death-song which Moses sang with the people (Deut. xxxiii. 2), it is said, "He came with ten thousand of his saints," or holy ones; and still again, "The chariots of God are twenty thousand, even thousands of angels." The martyr Stephen also, in his address before the Sanhedrim, says that they "received the law by the disposition of angels." Acts vii. 53.

It seems, therefore, that the great King paid this visit to his people attended by a great retinue, but from the silence of the original narrative on the subject it is probable that these attendants were not visible to the people. Moses saw them, but only when he went up into the mount where God was.

This agrees with the general plan of this remarkable theophany. While God indeed came down in sight of the people and spake to them for a time without a mediator, still, Moses was made his special messenger, and was admitted to extraordinary intimacy with the great King.

This intimacy is somewhat illustrated in certain events which transpired directly after the giving of the law. Moses was called up into the mount and bidden to bring with him Aaron his brother. "And Moses drew near unto the thick darkness where God was." The thunder and the fire and the trumpet voice had ceased, but the dark cloud still rested on the mountain, as the tabernacle of the God of Israel.

The errand on which Moses was thus called up was to receive for the people certain precepts by which the general law might be practically applied, and in which their duties should be pointed out in detail. These precepts begin near the close of the twentieth chapter of Exodus, and extend nearly through the three chapters following. They wind up with a series of promises and encouragements, well suited to reassure the people after the solemn display which they have witnessed.

In these promises it is once more said that God

is bringing them into the good land (Ex. xxiii. 23), and on condition that they shall use vigorous measures against the idolatry of the country they are assured of the divine blessing. Particularly, God says, "Mine Angel shall go before thee," meaning the pillar of cloud and of fire that had thus far led them on. "This is the Angel," says Stephen, "which was with the church in the wilderness" (Acts vii. 38), meaning the Son of God. And so, comparing passage with passage, we find that this Angel, this Pillar of cloud, this Jehovah, and the Son of God, were the same. He who tabernacled in the cloud dwelt afterward in human flesh. He who was with the church in the wilderness is with his people everywhere.

When Moses brought down these precepts and promises, he immediately made arrangements for a solemn ratification of the choice the people had made when they elected the Lord their God and King. Ex. xxiv. 3–8. He told the people what the law of the kingdom would be, and they answered in the accustomed formula, "All that the Lord hath spoken will we do, and be obedient." Then, to leave no room for future dispute as to what the law required, he wrote it out in a book; and all being ready, a day was agreed upon when they should enter into a solemn covenant with the King whom they had chosen.

This was, perhaps, the very next day after the giving of the law. At any rate, it was while the scene was fresh in mind, and the occasion was marked by several noticeable peculiarities. One was the building of an altar under the hill, or at the foot of the mountain. Moses had built an altar previously. It stood down in the valley where he had fought the Amalekites. But that was a merely monumental structure, and, so far as we know, was never used for sacrifices. This one under the hill, however, is to serve its full purpose; and as in those days all solemn treaties and covenants were ratified by the shedding of blood, this covenant altar was to receive a sacrifice.

The people understood this, and would feel the force of the covenant the more if it were confirmed in this way.

Another peculiarity of the transaction was the erecting of twelve pillars not far from the altar, probably between it and the congregation. These represented the twelve tribes, and probably consisted of some rudely-shaped stones. Then came the sacrifices—" peace offerings" they were called, because they ratified the peace between

God and his people. The offerings were made by certain "young men," probably persons appointed by Moses for the occasion. The new priesthood had not yet been established, and the old patriarchal priesthood would not have been designated "young men," but "elders." The sacrifices were oxen. It is not stated how many, but probably one for each tribe. Great care was taken to preserve the blood of these offerings, half of it being kept in basins and the other half sprinkled upon the altar. The altar represented God; and when the blood was sprinkled upon it, the divine side of the covenant was sealed. That was God's pledge to be for ever true to the engagement into which he now entered with the people. Then the other half of the blood was brought out, and the book in which Moses had written the law was carefully read in their hearing. Then again the people answered, "All that the Lord hath spoken we will do." Last of all, Moses sprinkled the remaining blood upon both the book and the people, saying, "Behold the blood of the covenant," and the transaction was completed.

It corresponds to this when our Saviour says, "This cup is the *new* covenant in *my* blood." 1 Cor. xi. 25. The old covenant was one of great solemnity; how much more the Christian covenant, sealed as it is with the blood of the Son of God!

When this transaction was past, Moses prepared to ascend the mount again. He was now ordered not only to take Aaron with him, but Nadab and Abihu, his two sons, and "seventy men of the elders of Israel." Ex. xxiv. 1. This was preparatory to a most extraordinary theophany, or visible appearance of God.

Those rude and primitive people had no conception of a really spiritual being. Their idea was that, although they had never yet seen their God, he dwelt somewhere within the mysterious folds of that cloud which rested on Mount Sinai; and as they saw his mighty works and heard his voice, they became possessed of a passionate eagerness to behold his form. It was against this feeling that Moses had to contend when he set bounds about the mountain, and it was against this that those extraordinary precautions were taken, lest they should break through to "gaze." The Egyptian gods could all be seen; why might not Israel, now that the covenant had been ratified, be indulged with one sight of their God and King?

It was to accommodate this powerful feeling

that the large company just described were called up into the mountain. Though God would not come forth from his tent in sight of the people, he invited these persons to come as guests into his presence and sit down at his table. "Then went up Moses and Aaron, Nadab and Abihu, and seventy of the elders of Israel; and they saw the God of Israel. And there was under his feet as it were a paved work of a sapphire stone, and as it were the body of heaven in his clearness. And upon the nobles of the children of Israel he laid not his hand. Also they saw God, and did eat and drink." Ex. xxiv. 9–11.

We tremble as we read these words. It may be that we shall stumble in the interpretation of them. But of one thing we may be assured: the great desire of that people was met here, and in such a way as to satisfy their rude sense-conception—"they saw God." We may judge that it was the same as the other more distinctly marked theophanies of the old dispensation. God the Son, who was to appear in human flesh, anticipated his incarnation, and presented himself in great glory before them. The circumstance that he laid not his hand on them is mentioned, as signifying that they received no harm. They had gone through the bounds set around the mount. They had gone up far enough upon the mountain to be enveloped in at least the skirts of the cloud. They had come into the presence of the hidden God, had beheld his awful form and had been seated as guests at the King's table. All this, and they were still alive!

Moses and Joshua went still farther up the mount, penetrating to the more interior depths of the cloud, as guests invited to "the secret place of the Most High." Even Joshua, however, did not go so far in that direction as Moses, but waited on some eminence there, while the latter climbed to a still more towering pinnacle, where he received the Ten Commandments, on the two tables of stone, written by the finger of God.

XXXII.

THE FIRST GREAT REVOLT.

THE first six days of Moses' time, after he and Joshua left the rest of their company and went farther up the mount, are not accounted for. We only know that "the glory of the Lord" abode on the mount, and that the sight of that glory was "as devouring fire on the top of the mount, in the eyes of the children of Israel." Ex. xxiv. 16, 17.

On the seventh day, however, which was probably the Sabbath, a Voice called to Moses; and, leaving Joshua, he pushed his way upward into those awful recesses, and reached the spot from which he was to receive a new series of communications from God. When he arrived there, it would seem that the extraordinary phenomena of the occasion disappeared, and that only the usual pillar of cloud was seen upon the mountain. Moses remained there forty days. Joshua waited for him where Moses had left him. The seventy elders and Aaron and Nadab and Abihu returned to the camp. Aaron and Hur took Moses' place in the camp, and soon things subsided into the ordinary routine.

No intimations having been given how long Moses would be absent, the people naturally expected his speedy return. In all his excursions up the mountain hitherto, a few hours or at most a single day had brought him back again. But a week passes now, and still he does not appear. Some are becoming uneasy about him, perhaps. Others, perhaps, are saying in their hearts, What a fine opportunity it would be to get rid of him! But whatever is the feeling of the people, he stays on. A whole month has gone by, and he does not appear yet. Another month is well begun, and it is the same. Had they not better break camp and go on without him? He may be dead. Who knows? If he is alive, he will easily learn when he comes down what has become of them, and can come on and overtake them.

This uneasiness was attended by a feeling which, with our Christian education, we find it difficult to understand. It grew out of those sense-conceptions of God to which so much regard has been paid thus far in their training. They want to carry with them, when they go, some visible representative or symbol of their national Deity. We worship without such a symbol, because, with the conception of Christ, the God incarnate, in mind, we are sufficiently provided with a likeness of the Invisible. But those people had had no such training as ours, nor had they any very clear conceptions of the incarnation. They had been reared amid the most attractive system of sensuous idolatry that the world ever saw; and for one of them to attempt to offer a prayer without a god-form before him would be like speaking into empty space.

This feeling is common to uninstructed human nature. Out of it grows image worship, that degrading system which it was the mission of the children of Israel to correct and cure. But the feeling could not be extirpated at once, and God did not attempt any such violence. He constructed an order of worship to accommodate it. He gave them a symbolry that met the necessity and carefully guarded it against abuse. And it was the very business of Moses, during these forty days on the mount, to elaborate that magnificent ritual, for which there was such an imperative demand.

They are weary of waiting for him, however. Their minds are made up. They must move on their journey, and they must carry with them a god. So, gathering tumultuously around Aaron, they exclaim, "Up! make us gods[*] that shall go before us; for as for this Moses which brought us up out of the land of Egypt, we know not what has become of him." This was rebellion. Still, it was not rebellion in the gross form sometimes supposed. They had no idea of setting up the worship of another god in place of this King. That could not be thought of for a moment. There was no occasion for it, nor is

---

[*] Elohim, plural noun with a singular meaning.

there anything in the narrative that, rightly understood, indicates any such intention. They were simply determined to proceed upon their journey and to take their god with them; and according to their idea, this required an image. The exact point of their disobedience was the making of such an image after it had been so solemnly forbidden. The spirit of tumultuous disobedience, however, manifests itself in numerous particulars.

There must have been men in Israel to oppose such high-handed proceedings as were now entered upon. In the tribe of Levi, at all events, Moses had strong friends and the true God true worshipers. But the current set strong, and those who desired to do right were overborne; and when the case was brought to Aaron, it came as the demand of the whole congregation.

For such an emergency Aaron was by no means the best kind of man. His principles were good, but he was not bold and straightforward in defending them. Had the demand been made upon Moses, "Up! make us gods!" how easy it is to guess how he would have resisted it! Aaron was too much after the order of his progenitor Jacob: he never made a bold stroke when he could compass his end by strategy.

So, instead of meeting this demand boldly, he seems like one attempting a trick upon them. Give me your jewels (Ex. xxxii. 2), he says; nothing will answer to make a god of but gold, and it must be gold that has been once cast into jewels. Give me those earrings that you prize so highly, memorials of your escape from the Egyptian captivity. That, he probably thought, was a master-stroke. "Can a maid forget her ornaments, or a bride her attire?" The jewels will never be given up, he thinks, and here will be the end of this disagreeable business.*

But such men as Aaron are frequently quite ignorant of human nature, and in this case he had made one mistake. He had underestimated the popular feeling, and, to his horror no doubt, the earrings were promptly brought and laid at his feet. Still, however, there is a chance for him. A sagacious man should not be baulked by one error, and if he can contrive a little delay, all may come out right, even yet. He is entitled, of course, to a little time for the casting and shaping of the image; and as all such objects were dedicated with a festival, he can, perhaps, gain a few days more by arranging wisely for that. Before matters progress too far, perhaps,

* Smith's O. T. Hist., page 172.

Moses will appear, and then he will turn the business over into his hands.

So he proceeds to make a god. They call it a calf. It is after the fashion of a famous Egyptian god called Apis.* That will be as good a symbol of deity as any, and it is one the people are accustomed to. It is called a calf of gold, but the gold is probably only laid on in thin plates on the outside, the centre being of wood or clay.† T

APIS.

work progresses slowly, but at last it is done. All is ready, and Moses has not yet come. To-morrow the festival will have to be held. It will be held as a "feast to Jehovah" (Ex. xxxii. 5), indeed, but it has such a shocking likeness to their former heathen festivals that there is some danger that Aaron cannot perfectly control it. What would he not give if, even at this last extremity, Moses would only come?

But the morrow dawns, and the people are making ready. Oxen are sacrificed and drink-offerings are brought, and they grow merry after

* Smith's O. T. Hist., page 178. † Kitto's Script. Read.

the old style. This is a little like it at last. Here is a god a man can make something of, and this is a sort of worship one can enjoy.

The drink-offerings soon began to take effect, and then came on what Aaron had all along feared. The festival ran into a carousal, and the carousal became a dance, and the dance, as was its nature, became lascivious. It grew to a high revel. There were singing and shouting, and frenzied men and naked women (Ex. xxxii. 25) were tossing their arms and making mazy circles round the golden god, when, just as the revelry was at its height, down came Moses from the mount.

He had been apprised (Ex. xxxii. 7) that something was going wrong before he began to descend the mountain, and it also appears that he had had a struggle in prayer on behalf of the people to turn away the divine wrath. But when he saw the reality, it was worse than he had anticipated. He found Joshua where he had left him on the mount; and when the two came within hearing of the camp, they perceived an uproar. They were not in sight yet; and as nothing had been explained to Joshua, he exclaimed, with true military instinct, "There is a noise of war in the camp." Perhaps he thought that Amalek had come again. But Moses answered as one who knew (Ex. xxxii. 18): "It is not the voice of them that shout for mastery, neither is it the voice of them who cry for being overcome, but the noise of them that sing do I hear." Then they turned a projecting point, and the whole scene was before them. There was the great golden calf set aloft on its pedestal, and there were the people dancing around it in naked frenzy.

Ordinarily, Moses was a man of the mildest spirit. Our translation of the Scriptures represents him as "meek above all men;" and though it may be doubted whether the word "meek" is to be taken here in its usual sense, yet this feature of his character is unquestionable.* Like many other quiet men, however, he was terrible when roused. We saw that when he killed the Egyptian. We saw it again when he drove back the shepherds who were doing violence to the daughters of Raguel. And such was his jealousy for the honor of God that a scene such as he now beheld would exasperate him beyond all bounds. Idolatry in Israel! Idolatry under the very shadow of Mount Sinai!

He had the two tables of stone in his hands

---
* Bush, Num. xii. 3, "abused."

when the scene burst upon him; but as he saw the people he hurled those sacred records upon the rocks at his feet and dashed them into a thousand pieces. Then striding straight into the camp, with the fire of holy wrath in his eye, he caught hold of the golden abomination, and hurled it upon the altar fire near by, as if he would burn it to ashes. Dragging it again from the fire, he threw it upon the ground, and then he beat it with fragments of rock till it was fairly torn into shreds. Then scraping up the mingled gold and ashes and clay dust, he cast it into the brook that ran by, and made the people kneel down and drink the water. Then putting himself in military attitude, he shouted, "Who is on the Lord's side? Let him come over unto me."

This call was promptly answered, and the response came entirely from the tribe of Levi. In that tribe the feeling had set strong against this whole business; and when they heard Moses call for help, they drew sword and rallied round him. "Go through the camp and smite," he cried. And they went, sparing neither son nor brother. They knew the rioters full well. They could distinguish them by their flushed faces, their disordered dress, and their wild hurrying to and fro. They also knew who the leaders in this business were, and they did not return their swords to their sheaths until about three thousand (Ex. xxxii. 28) of those wretches lay weltering in their gore.

Doubtless the camp needed this cleansing. That "mixed multitude" who came up with them out of Egypt, joining with the half-hearted and the wicked among themselves, had gained the ascendency. This slaughter reduced the disorderly element. To put three thousand of its very worst characters out of the way at one stroke would be a great thing for almost any nation. For Israel it wrought wonders. The offence had also been one to require severe chastisement. It was an offence that concerned their religion, striking at it in a vital point—the very point on which heaven and earth were being moved to establish things on a right foundation. And it shows that the lesson was none too severe, that before they left that encampment another judgment stroke had to fall upon two men who were of the faithful tribe of Levi itself. Lev. x. 2.

The fact was, that those people had worn the chain and cringed to the lash till something like whip and chain had become a necessity. They had proved themselves insensible to the higher motives which move mankind. All the way up to Sinai they had been coaxed and fondled and waited upon until that sort of treatment was about exhausted. Like rough boys at school, they needed a little rough handling, and in these visitations they were met at last by arguments leveled to their capacities, and by motives adapted to their mode of thought.

The next day we find Moses before the Lord again offering this broken prayer: "Oh this people have sinned a great sin, and have made them gods of gold. Yet now if thou wilt forgive their sin. . . . And if not, blot me I pray thee out of thy book." Ex. xxxii. 31, 32.

XXXIII.

THE PLAN OF GOD.

NO one can follow the children of Israel far along this strange journey without asking, What is being done with them? The answer may indeed be made that God is leading them by the hand of Moses into the promised land, and the additional explanation may also be given that he is taking them by the way of Mount

Sinai for the purpose of discipline. But the question naturally arises whether the divine plan does not embrace something of broader interest, and whether, in the training of this one nation, there are not some great designs for the welfare of the whole world. It is time that we seek an answer to this question, and we will pause in our narrative and consider it before following their fortunes any further.

God's plan is, through these Hebrew people, to regenerate the whole world. He has been pursuing that plan for more than four hundred years, and now at last its grand features begin to be visible. They themselves are little aware of it, but none the less are they doing the work. It is according to the promise made to Abraham; "In thee and in thy seed shall all the families of the earth be blessed." Gen. xxviii. 14. God, through a chosen nation, is to keep alive the true religion, and eventually to give it the ascendency among men.

He has chosen this nation carefully. He made a wise selection in the original stock from which they sprang. First, there was Abraham, a man of extraordinary character and of mighty faith. And Abraham is kept in discipline till he is an old man before God gives him children upon whom to impress his own character. Of these children, the most promising one, Isaac, is selected, and he again is kept under discipline a long time, as his father had been. Of Isaac's sons the choice one again is taken, and then at last a whole family are incorporated into the chosen race. The waiting was none too long. The sifting was none too close. Jacob's family were none too well trained for the position they were chosen to occupy in this great plan of God.

It was part of this plan somewhat to isolate the chosen people. "Israel shall dwell alone" (Num. xxiii. 9), said the prophet, and great pains were taken to effect this purpose. Palestine was an isolated country. The laws given the Hebrews were a constant hindrance to intercourse with the surrounding nations. And their sojourn in Egypt kept them separate even from the people among whom they dwelt. They heard there a language which they understood not. Gen. xlii. 23. They were in contact with a people who despised their occupations, and from the time their oppressions began, they were still more completely separated from the governing class in that country.

In effecting this purpose some things occurred indeed which needed correcting, but these were the subject of discipline by the way. In Egypt, though dwelling alone, they were tinctured with the prevalent idolatry, and so far as this extended it unfitted them for the position to which God was calling them. This had to be cured, and to cure them of idolatry, especially of such idolatry as one would learn in Egypt, was one object kept steadily in view during this journey. The very first motion they made in the direction of a false worship, therefore, was met with that awful retribution described in the previous chapter.

Idolatry, however, has a basis in a certain demand of our nature; and unless that demand were met, there could be no permanent cure. There is in us all a natural craving for outward representations of invisible things, and it now requires thorough Christian training to prepare men for a purely spiritual worship. For men in that primitive age—men who had deteriorated from the simplicity of still more primitive times—there must be either an image of God, or in the absence of that some contrivance to bring his existence within the grasp of the outward senses.

Hence the Hebrew ritual. Truth was not brought to that people in abstract form. It was represented in some sacrifice or acted out in some ceremony. The sinful condition of man was so represented, and so was the atonement of the Lord Jesus Christ, and so was the awful purity of God. All these things were put in tangible shape, and so brought within reach of their minds. A process was begun with them by which to give them an education, and so prepare them to educate the world. There was a contrivance to represent spiritual things by material forms, and the contrivance was such as to please their childish fancy at the same time that it improved their hearts and minds.

These people were kept in their special relation to the world until the grand consummation of their mission was reached in the coming of Christ. From that point onward the Christian Church was set to fill the same place, and it is of believers in Jesus, and not of Hebrews merely, that the apostle says, "Ye are a chosen generation." 1 Pet. ii. 9. These according to divine reckoning are the true "seed of Abraham" (Gal. iii. 29), and it is to them our Saviour speaks when he says, "Ye are the light of the world."

XXXIV.

THE GREAT KING.

WHEN a new nation is formed, it is an important question what sort of government it shall have. The Israelites have become a nation; are they to adopt a republican government, or will they prefer a monarchical one? Josephus presumed that this question would be asked, and to answer it he invented a term. He called their government a theocracy—a government directly administered of God.

Sometimes the people chose their own officers, as in the case of the Judges (Ex. xviii. 21), and in that respect the government was republican. On the other hand, there was the separation of the priests and Levites from the common people, a little as if it were intended to introduce an aristocracy. And then Moses' rule was personal and authoritative, in that respect representing a monarchy. But the government was not republican, nor did the priests and Levites constitute a proper aristocracy, nor was Moses ever saluted emperor or king. God was the Sovereign of the land, chosen such by the people, and this signified not merely that he was to be worshiped as their national deity, but that he was to be directly and continually consulted and obeyed as their emperor and king.

The government of the Hebrew people was a theocracy. When the people chose God as their sovereign (Ex. xix. 8), it signified not merely that he was to be the object of their religious worship, but their ruler in all temporal affairs. If Moses gave them an order, it was because it had first been given him of God. If they wanted a law, they waited on God to receive it. Lev. xxiv. 2. And an oracle was instituted among them to which they could resort whenever they desired to ask counsel at the mouth of the Lord. Ex. xviii. 18. Jehovah was king. All departments of the national government, legislative, executive and judicial, were under his immediate supervision, and all officers, from the highest to the lowest, were accountable directly to him.

No government like this had ever existed before among men, and none like it has ever come after it, and it depends very much upon our clear understanding of it whether we shall make our way through the many peculiarities of that people without confusion of mind.

One advantage of this mode of government

was that it made it impossible to forget God. This was important. The human race were rapidly descending into the depths of spiritual darkness. Nearly everywhere else upon earth, except among this people, the knowledge of the true God was lost. Indeed, that knowledge, previous to their leaving Egypt, was dying out among themselves, and it had only been restored by those marvelous theophanies which had marked their journey to Mount Sinai. But with God for their king this liability was for ever forestalled. It brought him within the range of their every-day relationship. It presented him as a Being with whom they had the most immediate and practical concern. They could not forget in Egypt that Pharaoh ruled the land. No more could they forget upon this journey, nor even after their settlement in Palestine, that Jehovah was king and God.

Another reason for assuming this relation was that it put them in a new attitude as respects the worship of false gods. To cure them of such worship and keep them close to the one only divine Being was an object kept in view in all their training. When God had been made their king, the worship of false gods would not merely be a religious error, but would be treason against the state. To worship such gods would not be merely the introduction of a new variety of religion—it would be setting up a rival against their king; and of course the reigning monarch would be expected to put it down with a strong hand. Some of the laws against idolatry among the Hebrews have been called severe; but if idolatry were treason, then, of course, severe measures against it were to be expected.

Even that form of idolatry which consists merely in the use of images in worship was met by this arrangement. Such images they were inclined to use even when worshiping the true God, and it was difficult to correct their habit. But if God were their king, they would at once see how important it was always to approach him in the prescribed form. When they had had any business with Pharaoh, they understood well the routine by which they were to reach him. There was a certain court etiquette which must be observed. For a man to rush into the palace rashly, or to salute the king in any forbidden way, would perhaps cost him his life. And so they could easily understand that God, who was their king, must be approached in the way he had prescribed. He had told them never to come to him in the use of images. It was not merely a rule of religious worship: it was a part of the prescribed court etiquette which all must regard who would safely and successfully salute the great King.

Still another peculiarity of this relation is seen in the enforcing of religious obligations by earthly rewards and punishments. This was a prominent feature of the Jewish faith, and it was well that it should be. Earthly things have great power over us, and this would especially be true with a people such as the Hebrews were at that time. The future state was dim, distant, unexplored; but when God spake of the fruitful fields, flowing rivers and rain from heaven, they could appreciate it. And as God was their king, it was suitable that his laws, like the laws of any other king, should have material sanction. It is no evidence that those people did not believe in a future state that God's promises with them related so much to this life. It only shows that as the national sovereign he ruled them by motives adapted to their minds.

In the same light we have several mysteries cleared up in what is usually called the Levitical service. All the people were subjects of the theocracy, but the priests and Levites were chosen out to wait upon the king. In all monarchies there is more or less of livery among court attendants. They have a regulation dress while on duty; and as these Hebrew people had

THE HIGH PRIEST.

a king now, it was suitable that the court apparel should be prescribed. One thing in regard to it must be that it should not pattern too closely after what they had seen in Egypt, for in Egypt everything was mixed with idolatry. Neither must it be left to their own fancy; kings never left such things to the caprice of the courtiers, and in this case caprice would be dangerous. So everything was prescribed, down to the minutest detail. When, therefore, we read how "God spake unto Moses, saying," and then follow on with a pattern for a coat (Ex. xxviii. 4) for Aaron, or a bonnet and breeches for some one else (Ex. xliv. 18), instead of turning away to exclaim, "Can that be a revelation from God?" we are simply to observe that the king is prescribing the court dress for his attendants.

So with the minutiæ of the sacrifices and offerings. These were gifts presented to the sovereign, and all such gifts must come in a prescribed way. The people must be orderly. In serving the king even so small a matter as having a place for the ashes from the altar was not unimportant. The lesson was, Let nothing be done rudely or in a disorderly manner when you are waiting upon the king.

When, therefore, you read how "the Lord spake unto Moses, saying" that when the priest offered a pigeon he should throw the crop and the feathers upon the ash-heap on the east side of the altar (Lev. i. 16), or that, when the people cut their hair or their beards, they should not "mar the corners" (Lev. xix. 27), you are to remember what is being done there. God is giving directions as head of the nation to a rude and unkempt people. In the education which they are to receive one of the first things is to induce personal decency, cleanliness and good order. A nation who are to be known the world over as God's people ought to appear suitably clad, and with at least clean hands and well-combed hair, and for their own good, as well as to make them an example to others, they must unlearn many personal habits into which as oppressed and labor-driven bondmen they had naturally fallen.

No doubt some of these lesser regulations had a specific religious significance also, but that significance has been often sought where it was not to be found. When any minute regulation relative to the person or apparel or good order appears in the Hebrew service, it is enough to know that it was a state regulation, intended for their personal improvement and prescribed by the king. God stood at the head of the nation to administer its government. It was his purpose to elevate those rude masses from degradation into which they had fallen. And to do that he had to give them very careful directions in regard to some very small things.

XXXV.

THE KING'S HOUSE.

NOT a great while after the adventure of the golden calf we see the people all busily at work. It is not for their advantage to be idle; and as they will not for some time resume their journey, the King finds them something to do. Here are men hewing out great planks from the stem of the acacia tree, or, as the tree was seldom large enough for their purpose, they were perhaps fitting together several smaller pieces into a plank, as the Egyptians sometimes did in boat-building.* Yonder is another company of men who have extemporized a rude brass-foundry, and they are casting the metal into curious shapes and polishing it to the very brightness of gold. Not far away from these opens a street between the tents on which the men all seem to be working in the precious metals, particularly gold, and the people are bringing to them great

* Rawlinson.

baskets of earrings to be melted up and beaten into new shapes. And last of all there is a great stir among the women, some weaving, some spinning, some engaged in curious embroidery. When the children of Israel went down into Egypt, they could not work at all those trades. They have learned something during their stay there, and they are now turning it to good account.

They are building a house for the King. They call it the tabernacle, and it is to be at once a royal palace and a place of religious worship.

THE TABERNACLE.

Two men (Ex. xxxi. 2, 6) have been raised up who are specially endowed for this work, but over them stands Moses to give directions, and Moses himself receives his instructions from the great King. The gifts for the work are abun-

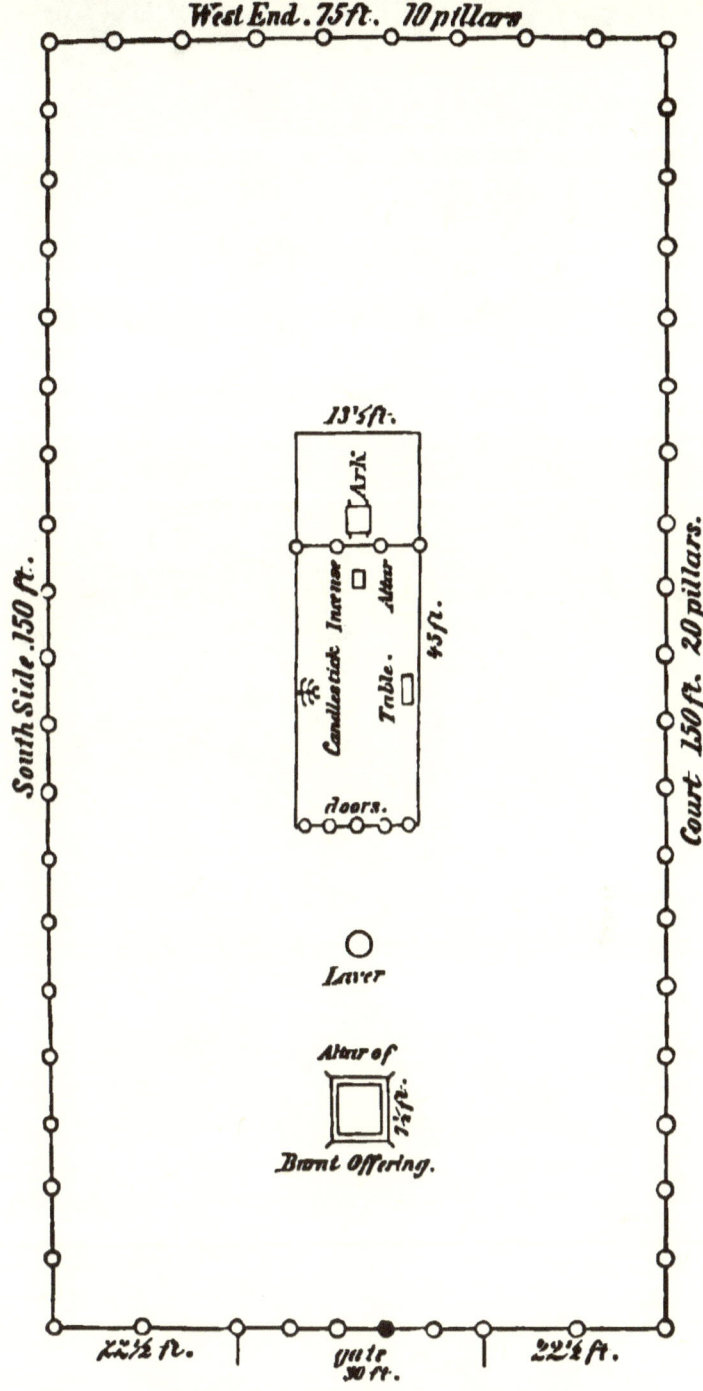

GROUND PLAN OF THE TABERNACLE.

dant, the labor upon it is diligent, and at last there it stands complete in its original plan. It was a curious building, very elegant in all its appointments, partly a house, but more a tent, easily taken down and set up again, and quite capable of being carried from place to place.

The walls, of precious acacia, were set in sockets of silver and hung with a tapestry of blue and gold. The ceiling, covered upon the outside with thick leather, impervious to water, was lined within to correspond with the walls. It was divided into two apartments by a heavy curtain, and there was a court round about, enclosed also with curtains in place of a wall. The King is coming to dwell with them, and they have done their best to build him a palace and give him a welcome and a home.

Of course the King must have his attendants, and to this service Aaron and his sons are appointed first, and under them the whole tribe of Levi. Everything about such an establishment, of course, must be put in the most perfect order, and so there is a place assigned to everything and everything to its place. When the people shall halt in their future journeys and pitch their tents, the King's house must be set up in the centre of the camp, and every tribe and every family must know its camping-place round about. And when they start on their journeys again, there must be men to take down the great palace and to carry its several parts upon their shoulders, each man knowing his part.

The chief of these servants of the king, all those admitted to his house and standing nearest his person, must be arrayed in splendid livery.

THE ALTAR OF BURNT-OFFERING.

Offerings must be brought by the people to provide meat for the great household, and that they may know that the king is there, they shall see him come in his chariot of cloud; and when Aaron goes into the innermost apartment of the tabernacle, he will indicate his presence there by a mysterious light always shining from above the mercy-seat.

Now, at last, it begins to seem to the people as if they had indeed a king. Now, at last, their God, though he "hideth himself" (Isa. xlv. 15,) is manifestly among them. And now, their government and their religion, uniting in one, take on substantial form, and the great truths they need to learn are dramatized before them. The beautiful house they have built is also a temple. The great king who rules them is their Creator and their God. And these liveried servants attending upon royalty are priests to offer sacrifices and mediators between the people and the Lord of hosts.

Many things, therefore, in this curious establishment had a kind of double meaning. In one aspect the priests were officers of state, in another aspect they were officers of religion; and as the religious aspect of the case, of course, was the stronger of the two, that grew upon them more and more, until the secular idea very much faded out of sight. At the beginning the tabernacle was the king's house. That was the thought first to seize upon their minds. By degrees the other view of the case grew upon them, however; and when at last they chose a king after the manner of other nations, the tabernacle was superseded by a more magnificent edifice which was simply and only a temple reared to the worship of God.

Some of the services of the tabernacle, even from the first, were unlike anything connected with mere royalty. Prominent among these was the continued requisition for blood. Aaron and his sons had to be inaugurated in the use of blood. Ex. xxix. 20. Blood must be sprinkled when the sin-offering was brought. Lev. iv. 6. And on the great day of atonement, when alone Aaron even was admitted into the interior apartment, blood must be sprinkled on the mercy-seat. Lev. xvi. 14.

This peculiarity clearly betrayed the religious significance of the royal service. It had an important relation to the doctrine of the forgiveness of sin. And though the people can by no means have explained it all, the principle became deeply rooted in their minds that forgiveness with God comes through the shedding of blood for man. Heb. ix. 22.

This was all they were at present prepared for. Under the influence of these tabernacle services generation after generation was to grow up, and the national mind was to be moulded. The king's house was more and more to become the temple of the Lord. The king's offerings were more and more to be regarded as exclusively the sacrifices of solemn worship. God dwelt among them; they must be careful how they lived. Their king was Jehovah, the great and terrible God.

XXXVI.

TAKING THE CENSUS.

THERE is one book of the Pentateuch corresponding somewhat to our modern census report. It is the book of Numbers, and it opens with the following words: And the Lord spake unto Moses in the wilderness of Sinai, in the tabernacle of the congregation, on the first day of the second month, in the second year after they were come out of the land of Egypt, saying, Take the sum of all the congregation of the children of Israel.

One of the important features of this passage is the exact date—the second month of the second year and the first day of the month. They had been one year and one month out of Egypt, and it was now, according to modern reckoning, about the fifteenth day of May in the year 1490 B. C. They had passed a winter in the desert; and summer being now upon them, and the business they had at Mount Sinai about concluded, it would soon be time for them to move. Before they marched, however, they must take the census.

One object in so doing was to prepare them for a military organization. They would enter the promised land as invaders, and would encounter the very fiercest opposition from the proprietors of the soil, and all along their march enemies would be liable to assail them unless they were well prepared for self-defence. They must immediately put themselves upon a war footing. Each tribe must have its captain, and the twelve tribes must be massed in four great army corps. Subordinate divisions must be created and officers of inferior rank set over them, and Joshua, as general-in-chief, must command the whole. The forces, all told, stood as follows:

Reuben	46,500	Simeon	59,300	Gad	45,650
Judah	74,600	Issachar	54,400	Zebulon	57,400
Ephraim	40,500	Manasseh	32,300	Benjamin	35,400
Dan	62,700	Asher	41,500	Naphtali	53,400

The total military force at disposal, therefore, was 603,550. This was a great army, but no nation ever puts its entire available force into the field at once, and it would be only in great emergencies that one-half these troops would be

SCHENCKZER'S GROUND PLAN OF THE ENCAMPMENT.

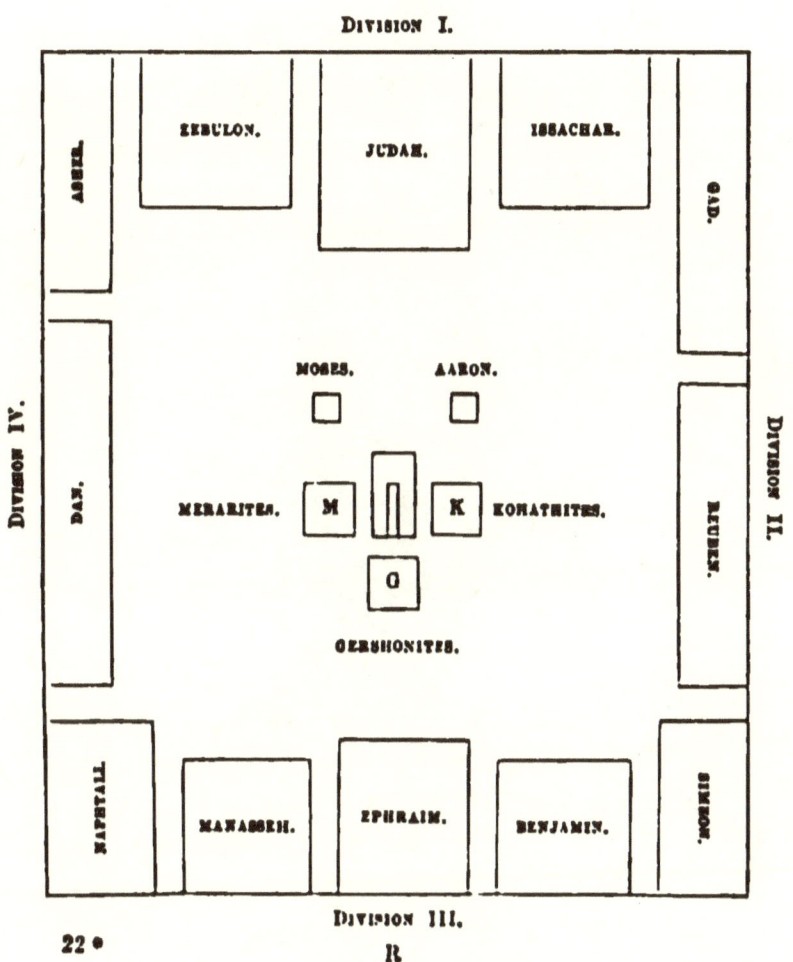

called into action. Often a mere detachment of a few thousand would serve the purpose, and the rest would be held as reserves. Still, it was important to keep account of them, to put them in training and to accustom them in their marches to military order and military law.

The four grand divisions of the army stood as follows, their exact camping-ground with respect to the tabernacle being specified: On the east and in the van were Judah, Issachar and Zebulon, mustering 186,400 men. On the south lay Reuben, Simeon and Gad, numbering 151,450. On the west were Ephraim, Manasseh and Benjamin, 108,100 strong; and on the north were Dan, Asher and Naphtali, numbering 157,600. The Levites encamped in corresponding divisions next to the tabernacle; and in front—that is, on the east—were the tents of Moses and Aaron. The following was the order for the Levites:

On the right encamped the Kohathites, numbering 8600, the count in this case embracing "all the males from one year old and upward." Their duty was to transport and take care of the ark, the table, the candlesticks, the altars and the other utensils of the tabernacle.

On the left were the Merarites, numbering in the same way 6200; and they had the charge of the pillars, sockets, boards and such matters, constituting the building itself.

In the rear were the Gershonites, numbering 7500, who were to transport the curtains, coverings, cords and hangings both of the house and of the court.

This made three divisions for the tribe. The fourth consisted of the families of Moses and Aaron.

These Levites had been separated to this special service in place of the first-born, and their cattle were consecrated instead of the first-born of the cattle of the other tribes. To make up twelve tribes after Levi was counted out, Joseph was divided into the two half tribes Ephraim and Manasseh.

Thus arrangements were perfected for the service of the tabernacle and for moving the great host without confusion even in the face of an enemy. Each tribe knew its place. Each man knew his duty. There were of course difficulties, in some of their camping-places, in perfectly carrying out this plan, but these were the directions to be followed wherever it were possible.

XXXVII.

ENFORCING THE LAWS.

TWO events occurred after the completion of the tabernacle and before their departure from Mount Sinai which were a solemn warning to the people. One of these was a judgment stroke upon two young priests (Lev. x.), and the other was the punishment of a man for profane swearing. Lev. xxiv.

The judgment upon the priests was upon this wise. Nadab and Abihu, Aaron's two sons, were set to burn incense, and "offered strange fire unto the Lord, and there went out a fire from the Lord and slew them."

It has generally been supposed that this "strange fire" was fire obtained from some common place, instead of being taken from the great altar. The fire on the altar had been kindled by supernatural means and was regarded as sacred, and it was probably intended to keep it constantly burning. This, and this only, was it proper to use in burning incense before the Lord, and the offence of these two young men seems to have consisted in using common fire instead of this sacred fire.

We are not sure, however. We only know that the fire they took was "strange," that they did as "the Lord commanded them not," that they made their offering in an unauthorized way, perhaps going back to some old-time custom of the days before the law. Whatever it was it was unauthorized, and they paid the forfeit with their lives.

This judgment stroke was a special warning to the priesthood. They must keep close to the law. Neither old customs nor new inventions must turn them aside from the rule. They must not presume upon their office to take liberties with the King. "I will be sanctified in them that draw nigh me, saith the Lord." Lev. x. 3.

Two circumstances connected with this event deserve special notice. One of these is that the relatives of the men who were destroyed were forbidden to express for them the usual signs of mourning. Even Aaron, their father, deprived of both these sons in one day, might neither cover his head nor rend his clothes. If he allowed himself to exhibit any of the usual signs of grief, or to approach those dead bodies with the common tokens of respect, he should share their fate. Men who had sinned in such a high place and perished under such a manifest frown of God must be given over by their relatives and buried like the dogs.

The other circumstance was a prohibition given immediately on this event concerning wine and strong drink. Nadab and Abihu are scarcely disposed of when the order comes to Aaron, "Do not drink wine nor strong drink, thou nor thy sons with thee when ye go into the tabernacle of the congregation, lest ye die." Lev. x. 9.

Had it been by wine and strong drink that these young priests had been led astray? It is not at all unlikely. Wine was one of the prescribed offerings, and in all such offerings the priest had his share. Nadab and Abihu could have access to wine every day, and their offering of "strange fire" is best accounted for by supposing them intoxicated at the time. Sacred fire was always close at hand. It never went out on the great altar. Why should they be at the pains to go away and procure "strange fire"? If we suppose them drunken, the question is answered; and if this offence occurred through drunkenness, we no longer wonder to hear it said, "Do not drink wine nor strong drink."

A man who exercised the priestly office must present an example of sobriety. If he used wine at all while engaged in his duties, he was liable to use it to excess. In such circumstances he should not use it at all.

Is not the same rule as good for the people as for the priests? With all the evils of intemperance now about us, ought it not to be our rule at all times, "Do not drink wine nor strong drink"?

The punishment of the man for profane swearing is recorded farther on. Lev. xxix. The offender was the son of a Hebrew woman, but his father was an Egyptian. The family seem to have been of that mixed multitude who came up with the children of Israel out of Egypt, and we judge by the story that the offender had no family of his own, but was a young man.

He became in some way involved in a quarrel. This was the beginning of it, and the quarrel became a fight. "And the son of the Israelitish woman and a man of Israel strove together in the camp." Quarreling and fighting go hand in hand with profane swearing, and while the strife was going on this young man "blasphemed the Name." Our translators have put it "the name of the Lord," but the original has it only "the Name." There is reverence in the record. The sacred writer would not even put down the word by which the sinner had cursed and sworn.

This sin had been strictly forbidden, but the punishment had not been prescribed, so Moses held the man under arrest until he could consult the King. When the order came, it was uttered in stern language: "Bring him that hath cursed without the camp, and let all the congregation stone him." Then a law was made that if any man among them, thereafter, whether he were an Israelite or not, should blaspheme the name of the Lord, he should be punished with death. Lev. xxiv. 15, 16.

This, being a purely Hebrew law, is of course not to be enforced under governments differently constituted. And yet it serves an important purpose for our times. It shows how God regards the sin of common swearing. It is a sin in his estimation worthy the severest punishment ever inflicted by man. Alas for the land in which this sin prevails! Alas for the man who goes down to his grave with this sin unrepented of upon his head!

23

XXXVIII.

BREAKING CAMP.

THE people had now been waiting at the foot of Mount Sinai something like a year. Num. x. 11. It was a year and two months since they came out of Egypt. The features of the country round about had become familiar, and their long abode in that one place had begun to make it seem like home. Many of them had doubtless strayed up and down the surrounding valleys to find pasturage for their cattle. The more enterprising and restless ones among them had climbed the heights in various directions and looked off upon the desolate scene. Every chief summit had become a familiar object, and Mount Sinai itself was like an old acquaintance every wrinkle in whose face was well known.

Not far from the first of June, B. C. 1490, they looked toward the tabernacle one morning, and the cloud that had so long rested upon it was lifted. This was the signal to resume their march; and however familiar they were with the scenes about them, they were doubtless quite willing to remove. So, while the tents were being struck and the tabernacle taken down, word was hastily sent along the valleys where the flocks were feeding, and soon the line of march was formed and the caravan was again in motion.

They had a religious ceremony for starting. When the ark was lifted, a trumpet was blown. Then Moses shouted, "Rise up, Lord, and let thine enemies be scattered, and let them that hate thee flee before thee." At this word the march began, and the long column moved slowly down toward the east, in the direction of the Gulf of Akabah.

This route took them directly past the home of Moses' father-in-law. At least this seems to have been the region where he once dwelt, for Raguel was now dead, and Hobab, probably the same as Jethro, had succeeded to the chieftaincy of the tribe.

When the head of the column appeared in sight, Hobab came out to meet Moses, probably bringing with him Zipporah and her two sons, and it was at this meeting that Moses gave him that affectionate invitation to join the expedition, which so well expresses the feeling of a true Christian toward the unconverted about him. "And Moses said unto Hobab the son of Raguel, Moses' father-in-law, We are going unto the place of which the Lord said, I will give it you. Come thou with us, and we will do thee good; for the Lord hath spoken good concerning Israel." Num. x. 29.

Hobab did not seem inclined to accept the invitation, and so Moses put it on other grounds. As we can do you good, he says, so can you be of great service to us. You are acquainted with the country. You can guide us along the difficult passes. You can bring us to the springs of water; and if there be any green places where we can find a little pasture for our flocks, you can tell us where they are. "Leave us not, I pray thee; forasmuch as thou knowest how we are to encamp in the wilderness, and thou mayest be to us instead of eyes." Num. x. 31.

We cannot be certain whether Hobab yielded to this urgency or not; but as he makes no reply to this second entreaty, perhaps we are to suppose that he accepted the invitation. Certainly he must have known that God was with the Hebrew people, and he could scarcely have regarded it otherwise than as a great privilege to cast in his lot with them and thus to become incorporated with so favored a nation.

So on they journeyed, still passing eastward, and following a succession of deep valleys that ran down from the high interior. It was less wearisome than it had been to climb up from the opposite side of the peninsula, but the country was very desolate, and they seemed at every step to be plunging into some new wilderness over which there brooded nothing but famine, and on which there rested the curse of God. They endured it for three days (Num. x. 33), when, perhaps overwearied, they halted, apparently for rest, and once more went into camp.

This was their first stage from Sinai. The place where they camped received the name Taberah, but was afterward called Kibroth-hattaavah.

XXXIX.

MURMURINGS.

THE word Taberah means a burning, and the other word, Kibroth-hattaavah, may be freely rendered the place of the graves. These are significant words, commemorating sad events in the history of the Hebrew people.

At this new halting-place the first thing we hear of the people is that they complained, and that it displeased the Lord. Num. xi. 1. What they complained of is not stated. Perhaps it was of the weariness of the journey; for having been resting in camp for a year, traveling was new business for them. Perhaps, on the other hand, they complained that the march was not made more rapidly, for they were only making ten or twelve miles a day; and how long would it be at that rate before they reached the promised land? Perhaps their trouble related to the character of the country they were passing through, for it was gloomy and desolate beyond anything they had yet seen, even in that great and terrible desert. But whatever the occasion of their murmurings might have been, the spirit they indulged was wrong, and the anger of the Lord was kindled against them.

Every outbreak after leaving Mount Sinai was met with the stroke of the rod, and the stroke in this case is described as follows: "And the fire of the Lord burned among them, and consumed them that were in the uttermost parts of the camp."

We do not know what this fire of the Lord was; we only know that it was a devouring fire to those who were exposed to it. And those persons in the uttermost part of the camp were probably stragglers, adventurers and hangers-on, embracing a large proportion of that mixed multitude who came up with them out of Egypt.

They were a restless and tumultuous class of people, and the troubles in the camp quite often originated among them. This breaking out of the fire of the Lord among them was the occasion of the naming of the place Taberah, the burning.

It is not stated how long they remained in this encampment, but it was long enough to witness another outbreak, originating with these same camp-followers and hangers-on.

This time the difficulty is described. They were not satisfied with the food that God was furnishing. "And the mixed multitude fell a-lusting; and the children of Israel wept again and said, Who shall give us flesh to eat?" That was the trouble. It began among the riff-raff and spread among the people at large. They were tired of their manna. "Our soul is dried away," they said. "There is nothing but this manna."

Now, the truth was that the manna was better for them than meat. It was a species of grain exactly fitted for their nourishment on such a journey and in such a climate. Moreover, it could be prepared in a great variety of forms, so that, at any rate, they might have been content with it for a little time, till they could get out of the wilderness and find for sustenance something more to their taste.

But when that people were once started in a wrong direction, they knew no moderation, and in this case the feeling rose till the whole camp was in an uproar. It was not so much an angry feeling, indeed, which prevailed this time, such as they exhibited when they were about to stone their leader. It was something more ridiculous and fully as provoking. They all, like so many little children, fell a-crying. There were not only tears shed, but there was loud weeping, after the true Oriental style. "And Moses heard the people weep throughout their families, every man in the door of his tent."

If it had been the children who had been making this ado, or even the women, it would not have been so strange, but to see those great strong men giving way to such a silly exhibition of feeling, and crying each because he wanted some meat to eat, kindled the anger of the Lord.

What a pathetic case they made of it! It had not been always so with them, they said. The days were once when they were better off than to live on manna. And running up to a climax in the enumeration of the good things they once had, they said, "We remember the fish, the cucumbers, the melons, and the leeks, and the onions, and the garlic." Brave soldiers, these, crying for an onion!

We have several times noticed how much like little children these people were; here we have it again. They are crying children, dainty children, children determined to have something to eat which is not good for them. So Moses regards them. "Have I begotten all these people," he says, "that I should carry them in my bosom as a nursing father?" And in the supremacy of his disgust at their conduct he prays God either to help him or kill him outright, and not let him be plagued with such nonsense any longer.

Moses is angry. He speaks words which his more serious judgment will never justify. But he is terribly tried, and the great and gracious God forgives him. Indeed, he makes arrangements to relieve Moses even before he attends to the people. He tells him to appoint seventy men to assist him, and promises to "put his spirit upon them." This means that he will communicate with them directly as he does with Moses himself. This was what was needed. Officers had been appointed at Mount Sinai by advice of Jethro, but they were not inspired men, and in those cases continually occurring which required communication with the great King Moses had to do the whole work. In a theocratic government that was too heavy a burden for one man, and Moses was breaking down under it. Seventy helpers, inspired like himself, would relieve him.

These seventy were accordingly chosen; and being brought to the door of the tabernacle, the Spirit came upon them, and they prophesied. Two of their number, however, for some cause did not come to the tabernacle, and the Spirit came upon them in the camp. This quite startled the beholders, and even Joshua, when he heard of it, begged Moses to call them to order. Moses, however, was only too glad of the occurrence, and exclaimed, "Would God the Lord's people were all prophets, and that he would put his Spirit upon them!"

This arrangement being thus perfected, attention was at once given to the people. A strong wind rose from the east, bringing with it an immense flock of birds. They had probably been blown across the gulf; and settling down with weary wing all around the camp, they were easily taken. Even those that kept up the flight flew very low, "as it were two cubits high" (Num. xi. 31), and were caught on the wing. The people kept catching them all night. They brought them in by the basketful. And now they fell to devouring them.

Of course immoderate indulgence in a kind of food which they had not tasted for so long a time, and all this in the heat of midsummer, was perilous. But as they had been children in crying for meat, so now they were children in eating it, and they gorged themselves till they could eat no more.

The effect was apparent even before the feast was ended, and afterward it became frightful. A terrible sickness broke out among them, the nature of which we can easily surmise, and soon they are dying on every hand. How many victims the pestilence swept off we can only guess, since we are not told—probably some thousands; and as they carried them out and buried them, Moses gave a new name to the spot. And he called that place Kibroth-hattaavah, the place of the graves.

Kibroth-hattaavah is one of the places which modern research would seem to have identified with some degree of certainty, and it is more than possible that among the discoveries of Mr.

Palmer* are certain remains of the very encampment of the Israelites we have just been describing. He finds an elevated spot of ground about a day's journey from Hudherah (Hazeroth), where, at some very ancient day, there evidently was an immense encampment. He describes the huge stone fireplaces with the marks of fire still upon them, and says he dug up pieces of charcoal, the remains of their fires, in great abundance. These remains extend over several miles, and at one or two points they are such as to show where persons of prominent position, perhaps leaders in the camp, pitched their tents, while just outside the encampment are a number of those heaps which could be nothing else but graves. Tradition uniformly points to this spot as the camping-place of a large pilgrim caravan, who in remote ages pitched their tents here on their way to Hudherah, and who were soon after lost in the desert of Tih and never heard of again. Mr. Palmer made a second visit to the spot, which fully confirmed him in the opinion that here, at least, are real traces of the Exodus, and that this is Kibroth-hattaavah, the place of the graves.

Sometimes a place of graves is a place of the

---

* Palmer's Exodus, page 212 and 262.

dearest and tenderest interest. But it was not so here. That broad burying-ground was the monument of the sensuality of an unmanly people and a token of the curse of God. Once burned with fire, it was now blasted by a pestilence from the same awful hand. The next move brought them to Hazeroth, the modern Hudherah.

XL.

A FAMILY QUARREL.

A MERE family quarrel may seem hardly worth the mention in the history of a public character like Moses, but domestic affairs and state affairs are sometimes very intimately related. Moreover, in this case the quarrel is in the family of Moses himself.

Hitherto, whatever the people at large may have done, Moses had been able to count upon the sympathy and the co-operation of his brother and sister. True, Aaron failed him sadly in the matter of the golden calf, but that was under a strong pressure, and he recovered himself again as soon as Moses was once more at his side. And now that he has been put under a solemn consecration as high priest, and especially now that he has so recently been afflicted in the awful death of his two sons, we should hardly expect to find him in a contentious mood, least of all disposed to be contentious with his brother.

But, strange as it may seem, he begins a quarrel, and Miriam joins him. Or was it not rather the sister who began the quarrel, and was not Aaron enticed into it by her? Her name stands first in the story. Num. xii. 1, 2. And Miriam and Aaron spake against Moses because of the Ethiopian woman whom he had married. And they said, Hath the Lord spoken by Moses only? Hath he not also spoken by us?

What does this mean? Moses was married forty years ago. Are they intending to bring up against him a matter of so long standing as that? This Ethiopian woman, or Cushite, as they contemptuously called her, is no second wife, but the same Zipporah, daughter of Raguel, of whom we have had an account. Is there anything to be said against her? Then by what sort of odd association do they join her name with the other cause of their complaint? Suppose that Miriam and Aaron have the prophetic gift which they claim, has Zipporah anything to do with that?

There is some mystery in the case. Family quarrels are generally great mysteries. Let us see if we can unravel it.

Zipporah has probably just come into the camp. Heretofore she has been with her brother Hobab; for though she paid her husband a visit soon after his coming up to Mount Sinai, she seems to have returned with her brother to wait till the caravan should pass that way. Quite recently they have met Hobab, and Zipporah probably came with him to join her husband in the journey.

Miriam's position as Moses' sister was evidently one of some honor. We see this in her leading the exercises connected with the celebration at the crossing of the Red Sea. But now that Moses' wife has come, a younger woman and perhaps a handsomer one, and the daughter of a chieftain in those parts, Miriam, of course, has to give place. This accounts for Miriam's trouble and shows how it might be that Zipporah should be flouted at as a Cushite. As to Aaron, perhaps something of the same kind has occurred with him on account of the presence of Hobab, her brother, who is probably in camp with her. So Miriam begins to talk and Aaron falls in with her, and the two make common cause.

One imagines the two in council. Aaron is a man a little like Jacob, and given to compassing his ends by strategy. He proposes to talk down Moses' wife. She is not a Hebrew. That will be a good point to make. What has she to do taking things over Miriam's head? Is the great prophetess to succumb to a Cushite? Is that Cushite family to put itself at the head of affairs? Israelites should govern Israel! That will make a capital war-cry.

We cannot tell whether Aaron said just this, but it is what he would be likely to say, and as he was an eloquent man, when once he began upon this theme, perhaps he talked Miriam into more of a passion than he intended. Besides, Miriam had a tongue of her own, and it may be could use it as effectively as her brother.

When this kind of talk had spread far enough to reach Moses' ear, he took the prudent course and said nothing. But matters directly came to such a crisis that something must be done. So God himself interposed, and his voice was heard, saying, "Moses, Aaron, Miriam, ye three, come out to the door of the tabernacle of the congregation." As they went out in obedience to this summons, the pillar of cloud which usually hung above the tabernacle slowly descended and stood at the door. It was the signal that the King had a communication to make, and they silently waited to hear it.

Ordinarily the high priest went into the tabernacle to receive these messages. But now this is not allowed. God speaks to them where they are. He says nothing about the Ethiopian woman; that was not worth mentioning. He sweeps aside all that sort of pretence, and goes straight to the heart of the trouble. Num. xii. 6–8. Are these people going to submit themselves or not to his constituted agent, Moses? Their position has indeed always been an honorable one in Israel, but will they pretend that Moses has not always been kept above them? Even with respect to those prophetic gifts on which they pride themselves, do they not know that Moses' communications with God have been far more intimate and personal? Wherefore, then, he asks, were ye not afraid to speak against my servant, Moses? Then, with some token of displeasure not particularly described, the interview was closed, and the cloud rose again to its accustomed place.

That such a communication should have overpowered them all we may well suppose; but when they had recovered themselves sufficiently to look about them, a sight met them that still more terribly affected them. There stood Miriam, the chief transgressor, a ghastly leper! Aaron was never a man of great courage, and this sight unnerved him. How did he know but the next moment the same blow would fall upon himself? What should he do? What could he do but turn eagerly to Moses and beg him to interfere in the terrible affair?

So down he goes on his knees before his brother, and shows about as much meanness in cringing and fawning as he has done of folly in the high words he has so recently spoken. "My lord Moses," he says—mark the words!—"my lord Moses, we have done very foolishly." That was the truth at any rate. "Lay not this sin upon us!" And Moses knelt there with his wicked brother and his smitten sister, and prayed God to take away the awful curse.

God heard him and gave what he asked. But there was a law in regard to leprosy which must be executed upon Miriam, even though she had been restored. Under that law she was put out of the camp for seven days, as one whose presence would defile the people; and when she came back, she was a less troublesome woman. Aaron had been sufficiently humbled by what he saw in her.

It was a very foolish quarrel, but quarrels are generally foolish. Its principal significance lay in the fact that it was an uprising against Moses. He was the divinely-appointed leader of the nation. Had this conspiracy been successful, it would have broken down all his authority. It was promptly checked and was never repeated.

XLI.

A LOST OPPORTUNITY.

IN the first chapter of Deuteronomy it is said that there are eleven days' journey from Horeb by way of Mount Sinai to Kadesh-barnea. But in the thirty-third chapter of the book of Numbers we discover that the children of Israel encamped no less than twenty times along that way. So the journey that should have been performed in less than two weeks actually occupied nearly three weeks, not counting the time they remained in camp at the several stations. Their haltings, in some cases, must have been of several days' continuance; for as they reached Kadesh-barnea at the time of the first ripe grapes (Num. xiii. 20), the summer must have nearly passed; for grapes do not begin to ripen there till about the first of September. From early June till late in August, therefore, they were slowly making their way from Mount Sinai to the border of Palestine.

A march of two or three days would take them from Hazeroth to that great wady which extends from the Gulf of Akabah to the Dead Sea, and which is called in modern times the Arabah. This valley they would follow still northward a little way, when their course would deflect slightly to the left, and they would pass up into the plateau of the Tih. From this point their route would be quite direct, every step bringing them nearer the promised land. They were still traversing a desert country, but it was not such a terrible desert as they had passed in the neighborhood of Mount Sinai. The farther they journeyed, the more numerous were the indications that they were emerging into a fruitful region. The stunted bushes now began to appear in the form of trees. Here and there they crossed little surfaces of grass, and these grew broader and were less dried up. They began to hear the voices of birds and the hum of insects in the evening air, and the deep silence amid which they had so long dwelt was broken.

For a part of this journey their way was quite

level, but toward the last they began to ascend a rising ground, sloping toward them from the mountains of the Amorites, and at length they were fairly upon the confines of the country which God had given them. Here they halted and prepared for further action. This halting-place was Kadesh-barnea.

The first thing to be done by an invading force is to obtain some knowledge of the country. So they selected twelve men, one from each tribe, and sent them up to spy out the land. They were to report whether it were a desirable country or not, and were to bring, if possible, some specimens of its productions. But their chief business was to acquaint themselves with the military resources of the inhabitants, and to ascertain by what routes and passes the Hebrew army could best push its way among them.

The men performed their mission well. They explored the country to the extreme north and learned everything that could be learned by personal observation in so short a time. Forty days were occupied in the expedition, and they all came safe back to camp, bringing among other things a monster grape cluster as evidence of the fruitfulness of the soil. They said that it was indeed a good land, but they gave their judgment that it was a country too thoroughly fortified to be conquered. "We be not able to go up against the people, for they be stronger than we." Lev. xiii. 31.

This was the majority report. Two of the spies, however, brought in a dissenting opinion in one particular. These were Caleb and Joshua, who not only said that the country was beautiful and flourishing, but gave it as their opinion that the military force at Moses' disposal was quite sufficient for its conquest. Here were above half a million men of war, and they were now thoroughly organized. The Canaanites, Amorites, Hittites and all the other tribes combined could not match that force; and, besides, they were divided into a multitude of petty sovereignties, and seldom acted together. Above all, was not the Lord God among the Hebrews? "Let us go up at once and possess the land: we be well able to overcome it."

This, of course, was a reproach upon the other spies, whose judgment and advice were so different. It virtually charged them with cowardice, and of course they were put upon their self-defence. So in reply they undertook to make the case as bad as possible. They did not hesitate even at the grossest exaggerations, but invented stories that were purest fictions, to show that they had not been needlessly alarmed.

The cities in that country, they said, were surrounded by walls that were built clear up to the sky, or "walled up to heaven," as they phrased it. As for the people, they were giants, and so much larger than common men that the spies seemed to themselves no bigger than grasshoppers by the side of them. And then, as if to give a dark hint as to the way in which these monsters disposed of any little people they could lay hands on, they added, "It is a land that eateth up the inhabitants thereof."

That was enough. They need not have gone so far. It did not take much to frighten those Hebrews, and these extravagant and ridiculous stories were all accepted as religious truth. The result was a great panic. Such terrible danger so very near them fairly deprived them of their sober senses, and Joshua and Caleb, who undertook to calm the feeling, were near losing their lives. Moses and Aaron, seeing how things were going, and understanding perfectly how useless it was to attempt to control a mass of men when such an excitement was raging, hurried away and cast themselves before the Lord.

Meanwhile, the panic spread till confusion was

worse confounded. They all fell a-crying. They wished they had died in Egypt. They wished they had died in the wilderness. They declared they would go immediately back again, and at last the feeling crystalized into the unanimous call, "Come, let us make us a captain; and let us return into Egypt." Num. xiv. 4.

This of course was a rejection of Moses, and equally a rejection of God. Mutiny and apostasy stood in the camp side by side. It shows how reckless and absurd were their conclusions, that they did not remember that they never could get back into Egypt without the continuance of the miracle of the manna all the way.

Things had reached a state at this point where some one must interfere; and as Moses could do nothing with them, God himself once more took them in hand. Suddenly the pillar of cloud came down and stood at the door of the tabernacle. As suddenly there began to flash out from its dark unfoldings an awful brightness. The people saw it, and knew that the King had come down and was about to speak again. We may well suppose, therefore, that the tumult was hushed for the moment while they saw Moses slowly drawing near the place where God was and waiting to hear his words.

The communication made to Moses was to this effect: This people had been rescued, borne with, instructed and cared for as no other people had ever been. They had been delivered out of Egypt, they had been taken across the Red Sea, and having been led through the desert, they had now been brought to the borders of a magnificent country which God had intended to give them. But what did it amount to? Not to speak of their frequent rebellions by the way, here they were, just where men of any courage would be stimulated to do their utmost, scared to death by a story that a nurse might tell to frighten children. Nor was it mere fright in them, either: fear had curdled into rebellion and rebellion into apostasy, and a settled plan had been already agreed upon to break away from God and undo all that had been done. Here this business should end. Every soul of this rebellious crew should perish right there on the spot. God would not bear this treatment any longer. He would sweep them all off, and take Moses and begin again and raise up a better nation.

It is now Moses' turn to be alarmed. This people have often tried his patience, but he has had them so long in charge now that he has quite set his heart upon them. He begs God not to be angry with them. He even proceeds to use arguments in the case, and to tell him how his own great name would be dishonored among men if he should cut those people off just then and there. And in spite of all philosophical objections concerning the immutability of God and the insufficiency of prayer, he succeeds. One thing, however, God will not change. Those people shall never have the splendid inheritance to which he has brought them. They must turn directly back into the wilderness from which they have just escaped and stay there till a new generation shall be raised up to inherit the promises made to their fathers. That coming generation, inured to the hardships of the desert and trained under the institutions of the theocracy, will perhaps prove themselves a worthier people. He will give them forty years in which to make the experiment, and then he will let them see again what they can do.

Moses rehearsed all this to the people, and the effect was to create a complete revulsion of feeling. It was all very easy to threaten to go back and to wish themselves dead when they were under an excitement, but when it came to the case in hand things seemed changed. That dreary desert again, and for forty years! and to wear out life there and die and be buried without ever seeing the goodly land! Nay, nay. They could not agree to that. And they fell a-mourning again, and then ran into rebellion a second time. They were not going back. They were going to march straight up into the country and conquer it.

So they organized an expedition and marched out. Moses told them that no good would come of it, and so it proved. At the very first sight of the enemy the poor cowards fled and came running into the camp, leaving several of their number slain behind them. Then the camp broke up, and they turned away from the green slopes of Palestine and plunged once more into those awful solitudes from which they had just emerged. They had had their opportunity, and it had passed away.

XLII.

A SABBATH LESSON.

BEFORE the caravan entirely disappears amid the desert shadows, two or three events occur which deserve notice. One of them is recorded in the fifteenth chapter of the book of Numbers, and possesses some interest for us, from the illustration which it affords of God's regard for the Sabbath day. The record says, "And while the children of Israel were in the wilderness, they found a man that gathered sticks upon the Sabbath day. And they that found him gathering sticks brought him to Moses and Aaron."

This case was very much like that of the profane swearer, already noticed. A law had been made against servile work on the Sabbath, but it had not yet been stated what the penalty should be. So they kept the man under arrest until the mind of the Lord should be known. "And the Lord said unto Moses, The man shall be surely put to death; all the congregation shall stone him with stones without the camp." Num. xv. 35.

This case has often been severely commented upon. To make it a capital offence to break the Sabbath, and to visit the death penalty in its severest form for the small matter of picking up a few sticks on that day to kindle a fire in some poor man's dwelling, has been described as the height of cruelty. We need, therefore, carefully to study the transaction.

"Gathering sticks" may indeed mean, as represented, picking up a few sticks to kindle a poor man's fire. But, as it may also mean something very different, why should we confine the expression to so small a matter? It may mean what our farmers would call " hauling a load of wood " on the Sabbath day, and it may not have been confined to one load or two. The man also knew the law, and knew that it was not a mere human law. It was but a little while since he heard it uttered by the mouth of God from Mount Sinai, and yet he defied it. This was a sin of presumption, and all sins of presumption under Hebrew law were punishable with death. Num. xv. 30.

It must be considered also that the act was an open one. The people saw it, and it was a very serious question whether such an act could be safely tolerated. It may have been also that he was a very prominent offender. All bad men are not poor men by any means, and the assumption that these sticks were to kindle a poor man's fire is quite gratuitous. This man was, perhaps, at the head of a prominent family—possibly he was chief of some clan. At any rate, infinite wisdom ordained his punishment, and among a people who always murmured when they could find occasion, there was not one who raised his voice against the punishment of this man. It was indeed a severe infliction, but we may well believe that something severe was needed just then to save the Sabbath day.

The Sabbath is an institution as much needed in this age of the world as it was in the ancient times. It was not a mere ceremonial ordained for the benefit of the Hebrew people at Sinai. Hebrew law indeed charged them to remember it, but it was an institution existing from the foundation of the world; and instead of being set among the mere ceremonies of that transient economy, it was proclaimed as part of the moral law that should be binding to the end of time. It is a day as sacred now as it ever was; and although we may not enforce its observance by the Hebrew code, we may, as a Christian people, enact suitable laws to ensure a proper respect for it by all the inhabitants of the land.

XLIII.

REBELLION.

FROM the first there had been an element of discontent among the children of Israel with respect to the authority of Moses, and nothing but the frequent interference of God in his behalf had kept him in his position as leader of the people. After they turned back from Kadesh-barnea this feeling increased. They made that movement sullenly. They were disappointed and in ill temper. They were angry with themselves, angry against God, and quite naturally angry with his immediate representatives, Moses and Aaron. In such a frame of mind it needed but the suggestion to make them believe that under different leaders they might have fared better.

The objection might indeed occur that Moses and Aaron always acted under divine direction, but that view of the case seldom had much weight with the Hebrews in their wanderings, They were always inclined to take that view of the relation of a priest to his God which we find among the heathen, regarding Jehovah as himself acting under direction from Moses and Aaron. Had they two chosen to prevent it, thought the people, God would not have been so severe with them. Had they not often controlled that mysterious power by prayer? Why had they allowed such distress to come upon the congregation?

This restless feeling was greatly aggravated by those institutions which had been given to them at Mount Sinai. A great change had occurred there in the management of their public affairs, and it was one that naturally gave great offence to the "influential classes."

These Hebrews had a great respect for ancient ranks and orders. We see a little of this even in Egypt, where, though they were crushed by a tyrannical government, they made great account of those hereditary chieftains among them known as "elders." These elders were first-born sons, or men from the families of the first-born. They made distinctions even among the twelve tribes in this respect, and Reuben's descendants, because Reuben was Jacob's first-born, were regarded as persons of high blood. The chieftains of such a tribe naturally stood at the head of the nation.

But in the Mosaic arrangement this order of things was quite disregarded. Even in the little matter of the order of marching Reuben was assigned a secondary position, and Judah was put in the forefront as the vanguard of the advancing army. And when the question of the priesthood came up, that honor, which had always been connected with the chieftaincy of the tribes, was carried off by Moses' brother, Aaron. As Judah took the front rank from Reuben in the order of the march, so Levi took the priesthood from him; and even in Levi it was not Gershon, the first-born, who came to the great honor, but Kohath, from whom sprang both Moses and Aaron. Ex. vi. 16–20. So there stood the two brothers, occupying the two chief places in the nation, yet belonging to what was regarded as a secondary tribe, and of a secondary family in that tribe.

Now we know that people sometimes cling to the supposed honors of a hereditary aristocracy about in proportion to their worthlessness. So when such an aristocracy among the Hebrews was superseded, though the change occurred by divine command, the circumstance created discontent. Any man of apprehensive disposition would have said, when he saw that arrangement made, Look out for trouble among the Reubenites of the tribes and among the Gershonites of the house of Levi. Those people have been put aside and others have been advanced over them.

In the event things occurred very nearly as this view would indicate. The Gershonites did not indeed revolt, but the Izharites did, who were Kohathites, as were Moses and Aaron, and the Reubenites joined them. I do not mean that any whole tribe or class was found in actual revolt, but that rebellion sprang up in just these disaffected quarters.

The Kohathites, of whom came the chief conspirators in the movement, were camped on the side of the tabernacle next to Reuben, and of course could conveniently hold correspondence with that tribe. It seems that there was a plan concocted at length to rally all the disaffected elements and make a bold push for a change of rulers. So we read, "Now Korah, the son of Izhar, the son of Kohath, the son of Levi, and Dathan and Abiram, the sons of Eliab, and On, the son of Peleth, sons of Reuben, took men; and they rose up before Moses with certain of the children of Israel, two hundred and fifty princes of the assembly, famous in the congregation, men of renown; and they gathered themselves together against Moses and against Aaron, and said, Ye take too much upon yourselves." Num. xvi. 1-3. There you have it—a revolt of the old aristocracy against the new régime.

Moses understood that movement perfectly, and he had measured its strength too carefully to undertake to breast it by any violent means. So he went, as he always did in his great troubles, and cast himself on his face before the Lord. He had doubtless seen that it would come to this some day; and had he been allowed to do so, we cannot doubt that he would have cheerfully surrendered the "little brief authority" which occasioned so much jealousy. But God had set him in the place he occupied, and till he was dismissed by the same authority he was not the man to desert his post. If the Lord who put him there chooses to defend him, he will abide. If not, he is not going out against the insurgents whom the old chiefs are rousing to oppose him.

One of the claims made by the malcontents is that every man is a priest now (Num. xvi. 3), and that there shall be no special priestly order. Moses therefore proposes that some of those who claim that prerogative shall go up to the great altar and officiate as priests, and see how God will meet the act. The two hundred and fifty princes who used to exercise that office can come in a body if they like. Let them fix upon a day—say to-morrow; and let them bring each man his censer with some incense, and let the Lord decide this question and indicate whom he has chosen.

They cannot very well object to that proposition; and so, when the morrow comes, the two hundred and fifty princes appear. At their head marches Korah the Izharite, and a great crowd follow. Dathan and Abiram have been served with a notice to appear also; but when it comes to case in hand, they grow nervous, and saying that they "are not going to come up for Moses," they stand in their tent doors and look out upon the chief actors in the scene.

While the princes are making ready, Moses, followed by Korah, who is either becoming alarmed or wishes to consult with Dathan and Abiram, hurries down to the headquarters of those two arch-conspirators to prepare for action there. "Stand back!" cries Moses to the crowd. "Keep clear of the tents of Dathan and Abiram." And the people surge back not only from those tents, but from that of Korah, just across the way. The conspirators themselves and their families are in their tent doors. Then Moses calls aloud and says, "Hereby shall ye know that the Lord hath sent me. If these men die a common death, then the Lord hath not sent me; but if the Lord make a new thing in the earth, and the earth open her mouth and swallow them up, then shall ye know that ye have provoked the Lord."

His voice ceased just as the princes waved their censers on high. There was a moment of silence. The next instant there was a lightning flash from heaven, and the ground was heaving beneath their feet. The rock opens in a great yawning cavern, and Dathan and Abiram and Korah go down. The princes are smitten with the seeming lightning stroke, and their half-burned corpses lie strewn about the altar which they have desecrated. Num. xxvi. 10. There is a scream of terror among the people, and then the ground closes again and the scene is over.

So ended the rebellion. So perished Dathan and Abiram and their families. So perished Korah, but not his family. Num. xxvi. 11. Korah, Dathan and Abiram were swallowed up. The two hundred and fifty princes were consumed by fire from the Lord.

XLIV.

NOT YET SATISFIED.

NOTHING is more persistent than wickedness; and strange as it may seem, these Hebrew people who have so recently seen a rebellion thus fearfully overwhelmed are again murmuring against Moses and against the Lord. Taking up the notion that Moses and Aaron have moved God to the severity he has exercised, they are everywhere saying, "Ye have killed the people of the Lord." Num. xvi. 41. It is only the very next day after the destruction of Korah and his company that this complaint begins to be heard. It spreads through the camp. It comes up at last boldly before Moses and Aaron: "Ye have killed the people of the Lord." It is strange that the Hebrews should venture on this new affront, but so it is. They will have to feel another judgment stroke before they are subdued.

As on the former occasion, therefore, God interposes. The cloud comes down upon the tabernacle, and Moses and Aaron go up to see what God will say. "Get you up from among this congregation," says the Lord, "that I may consume them in a moment." The divine wrath is thoroughly provoked. A swift punishment awaits the rebellious people. If they are in such sympathy with Korah and his company, let them prepare for a like fate.

But Moses and Aaron again fall upon their faces and entreat the divine mercy. The work of judgment begins with the word, however, and before the prayer has formed itself in speech death is striding through the camp. Moses perceived, by some token, perhaps by an outcry among the people, what was going on, and hastened to meet it. A plague had broken out on one side of the camp, and was traveling through it, consuming everything in its course. "Take a censer," said Moses quickly to Aaron— "take a censer and put fire thereon from off the

ANCIENT CENSER.—*From Montfaucon.*

altar, and put on incense, and go quickly unto the congregation and make an atonement for them." No time was to be lost, and Aaron hastily prepared his censer and ran with all his might to the scene of the plague. On, on it was moving, and the people falling, dead or dying, before it. Aaron threw himself between the living and the dead and waved his censer on high. Instantly the march of death came to a halt and the plague was stayed. It shows with what fierce rapidity it had spread, however, that before Aaron could put himself in the place to make the atonement fourteen thousand seven hundred of the people had died. Num. xvi. 49.

It does not appear that there was any further murmuring at that time, but the Lord sent one more sign to confirm Aaron's priesthood against all claimants that might come up afterward.

It was in this wise. Each tribe was to bring Moses a rod with the name of the tribe plainly marked upon it, and these rods were to be laid up for one night "before the Lord." In the morning they were to be examined to see if God had given any indication which tribe should take the high priesthood.

So the rods were brought up, and for the tribe of Levi they put in the rod of Aaron. The night passed quietly away and the morning dawned, and now for the test. A competent person was sent to bring the rods, and, lo! the one with Aaron's name upon it had during the night budded and blossomed and yielded almonds. Num. xvii. 8. From this they inferred that Aaron was indeed the man whom God had chosen. So there was never any further question raised on that subject.

Here we lose sight of the generation that came out of Egypt. As they pass down into the wilderness, however, we hear a great outwail, saying, " Behold we die, we perish, we all perish," and then we neither see nor hear them more.

XLV.

THE PLACE OF THE WANDERINGS.

THE general character of the peninsula of Sinai was given in chapter twenty-four, but the region over which the children of Israel passed on leaving Horeb, and the physical features of the country over which they wandered during the so-called "forty years," remain to be noticed.

From the foot of Mount Lebanon on the north to the Gulf of Akabah, which is the eastern arm of the Red Sea, extends a deep trench or cleft in the earth. In its general formation it is like the valley of Egypt—that is, it consists of a deep cut in the limestone rock on which the country rests, the walls on either side appearing as low mountain-ranges.

The northern portion of this valley contains the river Jordan and the system of lakes which that river connects. It is the most remarkable depression on the face of the globe, the river running for a considerable distance at a depth of more than a thousand feet below the level of the sea. The southern portion of this cleft, extending from the Dead Sea to the Gulf of Akabah, is known as the valley of the Arabah, and it is with this country that we are now chiefly concerned. For it was along this valley northward that Moses led the hosts of Israel when they passed from Horeb to Kadesh-barnea.

Following this track, they saw rising far above the low valley wall a range of rugged heights among which stood the famous Mount Hor. In one of the wild passes of this region stood the celebrated city Petra, with its arches, towers and temples cut from the living rock, and on the opposite side of the great valley lay the lower range, already described, broken through here and there by a dry watercourse leading up into the desert of Tih. Climbing this low range on the left, that desert lay spread out before them. It was a broad plateau, very uneven, and except in the seasons of rain presenting a naked surface of coarse, hard-beaten gravel.

They went up to this plateau from the Arabah, following some of the numerous wadys leading in that direction; and pushing northward to Kadesh-barnea, they stood at that place on the dividing line between this desert and the hill-

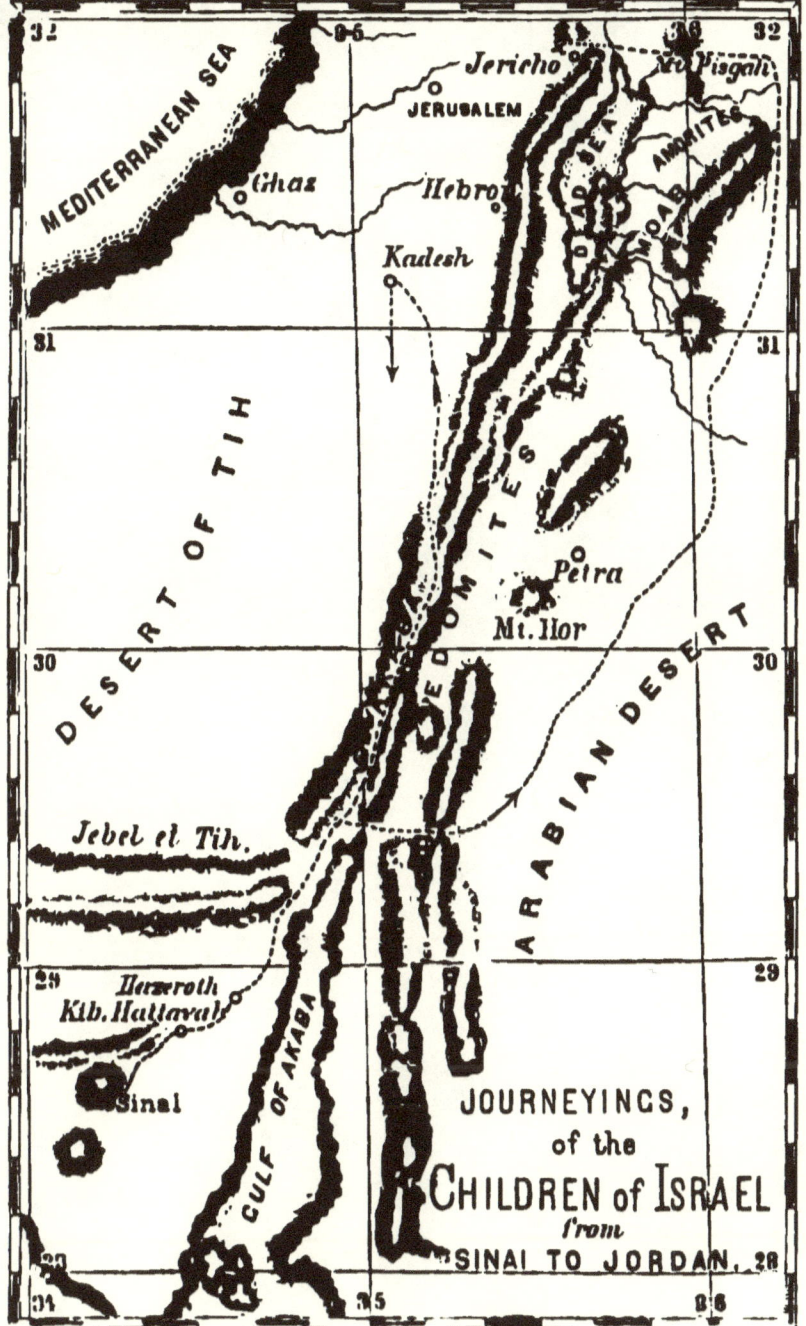

THE PLACE OF THE WANDERINGS. 309

country of Palestine.* That line, of course, cannot be very definitely marked, because it moves northward or southward according to the dryness of the season. Mr. Palmer identifies Kadesh-barnea with Ain Gadis, situated in lat. 31° 34′ N. and lon. 40° 31′ E., and makes a strong argument for his theory. It would be very unsafe to dispute so accurate an observer; but whether we accept his theory or not, we can at least approximate the locality, and the general character of the country thereabout is well known.

After they had been turned back into the desert the great plateau of the Tih was more or less their home. During the rainy season they found it springing up in every direction with rich pasturage, and if any year of their wanderings was unusually rainy, this plateau would afford them subsistence the year round. But if the drought came on, then there was the valley of Arabah, where they could find many deep ravines and secluded places where springs of water gushed out and where their cattle could find at least some scanty pasture.

From that great valley, too, they would quite naturally feel their way cautiously out into the

* Palmer's Exodus, page 285.

Edomite country, now and then seeking an outlook on their ultimate route to Palestine, and testing the friendliness of that independent power through whose dominions they expected to pass.

This, then, in general terms, is the place of the wanderings. Sometimes on the great plateau of the Tih, sometimes in the deep cleft of the Arabah, and sometimes pressing up the little wadys that opened eastward through the mountains of Edom, they exhausted the appointed time and bore the heavy curse.

Meanwhile, the old generation who came out of Egypt were rapidly dying off. Every encampment was marked with graves, and at the last, when but a feeble remnant of the old generation remained, Moses sat down and wrote the ninetieth psalm as a memorial of their melancholy fate. Moses, Aaron, Miriam, Caleb and Joshua—they five were left alone among a new people. The decree having been thus executed, they took the new nation to Kadesh-barnea and made ready to march straight to Palestine.

XLVI.

NEW ACQUAINTANCES.

IN the fortieth year of the Exodus (Num. xx. 1 and xxxiii. 38), in the first month of the year, or, as we should say, in the month of April, B. C. 1452, we see a great encampment once more at Kadesh-barnea. They have come up there apparently by the same route, and seem very much the same people whom we saw at that place thirty-eight years ago. Moses and Aaron are there, both much older than when we last saw them, but not so much changed as one would suppose. The tabernacle is there, too, and the same cloud hangs over it, and the tribes are disposed round about it exactly as of old. The Levites are there, their tents next the King's house, and their duties the same as they were thirty-eight years ago. And to complete the parallel, and show how perfectly the new generation fill the places of their fathers, the people are murmuring once more. Miriam dies and is buried here, but the solemn event in no way checks the misbehavior of the people. The truth is they are terribly disappointed.

At the time their fathers reached this spot the

country around was evidently very attractive. They must have come in soon after a fine rainfall, and when the ground was overspread with fresh grass. And as they were ordered back into the desert before the scene changed, the glimpse they had of the spot had always remained a charming picture in their minds. So they had always spoken of it to their children—the charming country of Kadesh-barnea. And imagination, dwelling upon it for long years, had painted it a very paradise.

But the new nation have arrived at the spot in a dry season, and the grass is all burnt, and where the streams should be there are only dry gullies and wastes of hot sand. They were in a better place than this when in the valley of Arabah. There, at least, they could find water and some sort of subsistence for their cattle. But here, if they remain, men and cattle will alike perish with thirst.

So they said to Moses and Aaron, much as their fathers would have done, "Wherefore have you made us come up out of Egypt to bring us to this evil place? This is no place of seed, or of figs, or of vines, or of pomegranates. Neither is there any water to drink." Num. xx. 5. Was this the fine place they had been promised so long? Where were all those wonderful fruits which the spies had brought into camp thirty-eight years ago? They had been cheated in a matter they had altogether set their hearts upon, and instead of escaping from the desert, they were dying of thirst.

So it seemed to them; and although we cannot excuse their conduct, we can easily understand their bitterness of soul. God understands it too and remembers that this is their first offence, and so he deals very gently with them. No judgment stroke falls upon these people, but, singularly enough, Moses and Aaron offended before the affair was over, and were both severely punished. It is a little difficult to understand the enormity of their offence, but as nearly as we can state the case it was as follows:

Moses was directed to supply them with water very much as he had done at Rephidim. In one or two particulars, however, his action was to be different, and his failure in these particulars brought him under God's displeasure. At Rephidim, he was to bring water out of a rock by smiting it; now he was only to speak to the rock. Num. xx. 8. But when he had brought the people up to witness the miracle, he smote the rock instead of speaking to it, and for some reason smote it twice. Instead of speaking to the rock, he spake to the people, calling them hard names. And instead of ascribing the miracle to God, he loosely spake of it as wrought by himself and Aaron. The two brothers united in the offence, and said, "Hear now, ye rebels! must we fetch water out of this rock? And Moses lifted up his hand, and with his rod he smote the rock twice."

One thing is tolerably clear—Moses was angry; and had we heard his voice or seen his face, we might have seen and heard more than we can now understand. To work a miracle in an ebullition of wrath and under an excitement which made him forget the divine directions—all that, in Moses and Aaron, before all the people, had to be rebuked. "And the Lord said unto Moses and Aaron, Because ye believed me not to sanctify me in the eyes of the children of Israel, therefore ye shall not bring this congregation into the land which I have given them."

What a blow! Both these men for one offence shut out of Canaan. After all their marchings to and fro, after all the burdens they have borne for that people,—after all that, these men, who have stood faithful among the faithless on so many trying occasions, fail at the last. Not the people now, but their veteran leaders, provoke the Lord and incur his heavy displeasure. They are not, however, consigned to the awful doom of that rebellious race whose carcasses fell in the wilderness. They are indeed shut out of Canaan, they may not enter the promised land, but their exit out of life, when it comes, will show that through grace they well regained the favor of God. Canaan is lost to them, but they have not lost forgiveness, hope or heaven.

XLVII.

DEATH OF AARON.

HAD it been intended to bring the children of Israel into the promised land from Kadesh-barnea by the shortest route, they would have proceeded from that point directly northward. In that direction a march of about sixty miles would have brought them to the gates of Hebron, and less than twenty miles from there lay the future Jerusalem. It was but a little way to go, but it was not the Lord's way, and the time had not yet come to go in and possess the land.

They turned back once more, therefore, and passed still again down the valley of Arabah.* The prescribed route was to bring them into the country from the east, and they skirted along the Edomite border, vainly (Num. xx. 21) asking permission to pass through, till they had almost literally compassed that land.

THE SUMMIT OF MOUNT HOR, SEEN FROM THE SOUTH-EAST.

Soon after their movement southward they halted under the shadow of Mount Hor. This lay upon their left, and was the principal summit of that mountain region. And while they rested here word came that Aaron was about to die.

* Stanley, Sinai and Palestine, page 84.

He was not sick, nor had he become enfeebled by age, nor was he to be smitten by any judgment stroke, but the event had been determined upon and the time had come. And looking at it now, we can see that it was a time well chosen. The office of high priest, so many times the subject of jealous contention among that people, was to be transmitted from Aaron to Eleazar, his son. The transfer was liable to be attended with disturbance, and it was well to have it made while the hand of Moses was yet strong upon the tribes. The new pontiff should take his office, and the people should recognize and accept him, while there was yet a man at the head of the nation whom they were accustomed to obey. So the change came then and there.

Some of the Old Testament saints died very grandly. When we think of death, we associate it with a sick-room, with feebleness of body and with mental decay. Or we put it in the more ghastly form of some destructive casualty, hurling men out of the world with mangled forms and amid scenes of confusion and outcry. Such dying is terrible. The grace of our Lord Jesus Christ can indeed carry us through it, but it makes wreck of our earthly grandeur and reduces our boasted magnificence to dust and ashes.

When Aaron died, it was in another fashion. He had not been sick, neither had his strength failed him. God called, and the hale old man went up to a mountain top from which he stepped off into heaven. There is no record of bright anticipations of the future world in the case. These were very little enjoyed in those ancient times. In such a case as Aaron's they were scarcely needed. Such consolations as these are sent to cheer our lowlier passage to the tomb. Aaron sings no song, utters no shout, makes no exclamation of joy. But, on the other hand, he shows no fear, but meets the event of death as he would have met any other great emergency. He takes Eleazar, his son, and Moses goes with them, and they three go up to Mount Hor to meet the great occasion.

When they arrive at the appointed place, Moses takes off the priestly robe from Aaron and puts it upon Eleazar, thus investing him with the office his father had filled. Then the old man turns his undimmed eye to the desert over which they have been wandering so long, to the encampment spread out at his feet and to the heights of distant Palestine, and bids the world farewell.

That majestic dying is enough to cover out of

sight all the follies of which the man had sometimes been guilty, and all the faults into which he had sometimes fallen. Brave old pontiff of the Lord's elect! We bow you a reverent salutation as you wave the world good-night.

The people did not feel much like journeying when they knew that Aaron was dead. The event cast a shadow on the camp. Now, at last, the old jealousy against the venerable high priest died away. Now they only remembered how he had been associated with their holiest services, and had been, through all their sin and suffering, their constant intercessor with God. "And they mourned for Aaron thirty days, even all the house of Israel." Num. xx. 29.

Aaron's death occurred in the month of August, B. C. 1452, in the one hundred and twenty-third year of his age. He was four years older than Moses, and Miriam was about ten years older still. They constituted together one of those remarkable families which sometimes appear in history, all the members whereof attain to great distinction. Aaron's native character was not solid, but grace triumphed over its deficiencies. Of his piety there is no doubt, though it was a piety sometimes disfigured by serious faults. The Psalmist calls him " Aaron the saint of God " (Ps. cvi. 16), and in all his later years he proved himself a fit companion for Moses, and stood well before the nation in the office to which the Lord had appointed him.

XLVIII.

THE FIERY SERPENTS.

WHEN the camp moved again, they went still southward till they reached Eziongeber, at the head of the gulf of Akabah. On the east from this point opens a gap in the mountain-range, and through this they passed toward the Arabian desert. Then turning short to the northward, they were headed once more for the promised land.

Their journey was as difficult, however, as it had been at any time during the whole forty years. They were passing through a country scorched and desolate; and as they were also climbing toward a higher level, the way grew weary and their patience failed them, and they began the old story of murmuring against Moses and against the Lord.

One complaint they made was of the scarcity

of water. Another complaint was that they had eaten the manna till they loathed (Num. xxi. 6) the very sight of it. And they asked Moses whether he had brought them out into that country to kill them.

This was their second offence. Their murmuring at Kadesh-barnea had been overlooked; but if this were passed by, they would take courage to murmur again. They must be punished, and the instruments of punishment were close at hand.

It appears that the region in which they were now encamped has always been infested with serpents; and except for God's gracious care, we should have seen them attacked by these poisonous creatures long ago. While they were obedient he let nothing harm them, but when they murmured he withdrew his protection.

So the serpents appeared. They called them fiery serpents from the fierce burning produced by their bite.* They appeared everywhere, crawling from under every loose stone and from every crevice in the rocks. They lay along the

---

* These serpents are often erroneously spoken of as "flying serpents," and so represented in pictures. The poetic expression, "fiery flying serpent," occurs in Isaiah xxx. 6 and xiv. 29. The epithet is probably given from the quick motion of the serpent when attacking.

footpaths, they came into the tents, and they saw them coiled for the fatal spring at their tables and on their beds. Nor was it the mere horror of the sight. People were bitten and were dying on every hand; and knowing full well what it meant, they flew to Moses for help from the Lord.

The remedy for this great evil was very singular, its meaning, however, remaining unknown till a thousand years afterward. Moses was to set up a brazen serpent, made after the fashion of those that had bitten the people, where all could see it, and all who looked thereon should live. Some of them might have had a glimpse of the transaction represented in this arrangement, but the very wisest of them saw but faintly what it meant. They would indeed remember, perhaps, the ancient tradition of the introduction of sin and suffering among men by the agency of a serpent in Eden, but the meaning of the symbol to which they were to look for healing was never clear to the world till One came and suffered and died, who said, "As Moses lifted up the serpent in the wilderness, even so must the Son of man be lifted up, that whosoever believeth in him should not perish, but have eternal life." John iii. 14, 15.

This brazen serpent was preserved as a relic among the Hebrews, and carried with them into the promised land. But when idolatry grew up among them in the time of the kings, the people had resort to it for forbidden purposes. Hezekiah, therefore, on coming to the throne, ordered it destroyed with the other images that had been worshiped in the time of his father Ahaz. 1 Kings xviii. 4. Such is the tendency of the human mind to idolatry that the most precious relic or the most beautiful symbol may be perverted to that end; and whatever has been so perverted, and been used so long and persistently in an idolatrous service, though it were the cross itself, were better laid aside for ever from among the visible symbols of our holy faith.

The punishment these people received for their murmurings taught them a good lesson. It seemed severe, but what right had they to claim divine protection when uttering words of violence against the divine King? They had not known, till God let loose the plague upon them, what powers of evil he was holding in check for their sake. They were taught henceforth to bear their sufferings more patiently, and were especially admonished that those who complain of the good things which God gives, as they had complained of the manna, will soon learn what evil things he may at any time let loose against them.

XLIX.

TWO GREAT BATTLES.

IT was not long after the plague of the serpents that Moses found himself emerging from the desert, with his hosts, and entering a populous and fruitful country. But it soon began to be seen that if the desert had its trouble, so also had the more favored land.

For they now began to encounter enemies. First they came upon the Moabites, that ancient people who had been driven down by the conqueror Sihon from their old possessions east of the Jordan to a region near the southern end of the Dead Sea. Moses opened negotiations with these people with a view to passing through their territory, but he was denied the right of way; and rather than provoke hostilities, he passed around upon their eastern border (Judg. xi. 18), as he had done with Edom. Then turning northward again, he pushed onward until they lay encamped at some point on the wide country far out to the east of Jericho.

Now, at last, he must pass through the dominion of a foreign power. Sihon's empire lay directly between him and the promised land. He could not pass round his border; he must have a passage through the land; and he courteously solicited this favor, pledging himself to do no damage by the way.

Sihon, however, was an Amorite; and besides his eastern empire, he held a province in Palestine—the country which the Hebrews were avowedly marching to conquer. So he not only refused to let them pass through, but came out against them to drive them back into the desert.

This brought on a battle, and Sihon, who had expected to route these invaders at the first onset, was met with a sturdy resistance. The Hebrews not only repulsed the assault, but followed up their advantage and assumed the offensive. After a desperate struggle the forces of Sihon were utterly routed, the king was taken prisoner and all his lands east of Jordan came into possession of the people of the Lord.

This was a great good fortune, and the people must have been highly elated by it. They had been refused the civility of a passage through the country, and now the country was their own. And a right fruitful country was it, too. Moses also must have been very much encouraged by this success. He could see by it how the military spirit had advanced among that people, and how they had improved in discipline by the steady drill of those thirty and eight years. So well appointed an army as that, and one that could be so well handled too, seemed somewhat suited to the sharp work they would soon find before them.

As Moses now led the caravan slowly down through that fine country, he encountered another enemy. This was Og, the giant king of Bashan. Rev. J. L. Porter, in his "Giant Cities of Bashan," shows us how strong an empire this king must have ruled, and with what propriety the term giant was applied to him and his race. Og had no business with Moses. His kingdom lay to the north, and it was not proposed so much as to touch the border of that country. But alarmed at the progress of the invaders, he took up the cause of his defeated neighbor and came down to intercept the caravan. It was just as before, however, for Og's army was utterly broken up and the king himself slain. And when that fierce battle was ended, a second kingdom east of the Jordan lay at Moses' feet.

It was well for the Hebrews that this conquest

was made. These repeated successes inspirited the army for the struggles that were before them after crossing the Jordan. Moreover, while they still lingered on the eastern shore, what a joy, to men who had so long dwelt in the desert, to drive out their herds of cattle to the rich pasture grounds of Bashan, and to pitch their tents amid the orchards and the running streams! Here, too, in military phrase, was a grand base of operations for an army that intended to move upon Palestine. Moreover, the fame of these repeated conquests would strike terror into the hearts of all opposers. A great thing was it for the Hebrews that these two battles gave them the country east of the Jordan.

That was so much more than had been promised them! When God fulfills his word, he does it generously. His promises themselves are large; but when the fulfillment comes, it is according to the apostle's word, "Exceeding abundantly above all that we are able to ask or even think, according to the power that worketh in us through Jesus Christ, to whom be glory for ever. Amen."

A CONJURER.

ALL through the Amorite country, east of the Jordan, were scattered the remnants of the race of Moab, the original possessors of that land; and as the Hebrews withdrew from the country, marching westward, the old king of Moab also came back to view his long-lost domains. His name was Balak. He came up from the eastern shore of the Dead Sea; and slowly following the retiring host, he began to think of reinstating himself in those dominions. Sihon was dead. If Moses and his people could be as well disposed of, Moab would once more possess the land.

How to dispose of Moses and the Hebrew people—that was the great thought that burdened Balak's mind. He had no military force to bring against them, nor, in his judgment, would such a force be of any avail. He has studied the history of that strange people, and believes them to be under supernatural protection. The great Jehovah God has them in care—that ancient Deity once worshiped even by Moab. His presence is continually marked by that cloud that hangs over their tabernacle. That people must be met, if at all, in the realm of the supernatural. The best plan of all will be to find some man, if possible, as powerful as Moses with the same Jehovah God, and match him against the leader of the Hebrews.

Acting on this suggestion, he begins to make inquiries, and directly, to his great joy, he hears of a man exactly to his mind. His name is Balaam. His fame is extraordinary. He professes to work by the power of the Jehovah God, and nothing against which he brings his incantations stands for a moment. This man lives at a great distance—it will require a twenty days' journey to reach him; but what of that? On this action hangs the fate of Balak's empire, and for the prize of a kingdom a man must be willing to play a deep game.

So he appoints a deputation of his princes to go and bring the wonderful man. They take with them a costly present, and are authorized to promise rewards still more valuable. They pursue their journey, led by the star of Balaam's renown, till it brings them into Mesopotamia. There the Hebrew race originated, and there they first obtained their knowledge of the mighty God. There dwells Balaam, and they soon find their man.

"Will he come," they ask, "and lay a curse on the Hebrews? If he will, he may judge by the presents already brought him how great shall be his reward. He is invited to this service by no ordinary man. Balak, who sends for him, is one of the ancient kings."

Of course it will not do for Balaam at once to answer that question. For appearance' sake he must affect to consult his oracle. So he says, "I expect a visit from my God to-night. Wait till morning, and I will see what he says. I am a prophet, you know, and in such matters can only do as I am commanded." Num. xxii. 8. So they wait till morning.

Balaam was a false man. He had no expectation of a visit from the Lord that night. That pretence was one of the tricks of his trade. But God sometimes takes the wise in his own craftiness, and Balaam was taken in his craftiness that night in a way that must have greatly terrified him. For, lo! the God whom he pretended to serve did indeed visit him, and gave him a message he was likely to remember.

So the poor conjurer came down to meet his guests next morning pale and sick at heart. "What said the God?" they inquire. The fate of the empire seemed suspended on the answer, and Balaam said, "I cannot go." It was all very well to play at visions and enchantments, but when the reality came it was a serious thing, and there never was a gladder man than was this conjurer when his guests departed and this business was off his hands.

The king was of course grievously disappointed when the deputation returned unsuccessful, but his all was at stake, and he could not afford to despair.

LI.

THE CURSE AND THE BLESSING.

SUCH men as Balaam were well-known characters in those days, and while the people had perfect confidence in their supernatural gifts, it was well understood that most of them had a high sense of the value of silver and gold.

The king of Moab understands this well, and begins to reason with himself whether a better offer might not bring Balaam to terms. So he sends again princes of higher blood, presents more costly and offers that ought to move all the conjurers in the land.

The journey is made again, and the business is

once more opened. Doubtless, Balaam is alarmed to encounter this troublesome proposal a second time, and so he cries out against it: "If Balak were to give me his house full of silver and gold, I could not go beyond the word of the Lord." That was a good thing to say, even if he intended only to keep up appearances; but remembering his late adventure, he doubtless spoke sincerely. Nothing scares a pretender like reality, and Balaam would rather meet anything than another such vision as he had on that memorable night.

But then there is the money. This great man loves money, and has never intended to be very fastidious as to the means of acquiring it. 2 Pet. ii. 15. It is for this that he has devoted himself to the gainful profession of magic, and this offer of Balak—why, it would make him his fortune!

He has heard nothing from God since the other deputation came to see him. Perhaps that will be the last of it. A man must risk something, at any rate, for so great a prize; and so he says, "Tarry here this night, and I will see what the Lord will say." Num. xxii. 19. So they all retire to rest, and once more, to his great alarm, the Lord appears and tells him what to do.

He may go with the men, says the apparition, but he must take care how he attempts any of his low tricks and false pretences in the matter. This is no common case, but one that God has indeed taken in hand. "Go," he says, "but God's angel will go with you, and you must not utter one word of curse or blessing except what is given you."

So he reported himself ready in the morning, and they made haste to perform the journey. But as they drew near the end of the way—the princes having probably gone on in advance to announce Balaam's coming—the ass on which he rode began behaving in a most unaccountable manner. The beast, always steady and docile before, baulked in the highway, as if scared by some object which it was to pass. Balaam saw nothing, and so, with some blows and perhaps a little cursing, he drove the creature on. It was an irregular progress, however, and at last, as if unwilling to proceed farther, the ass made a spring from the highway, landing himself and his master upon the open field. The great man gathered himself up, however, and got his beast upon the road once more, and went on till he came to a place where the way was fenced in on each side by a stone wall. There the beast again sprang aside, crushing Balaam's foot against the wall. There was another start, and a little more progress, taking them to a very narrow place in the road, when the ass fell flat down, quivering with apparent fear, and could not be roused to move a step farther.

Balaam was evidently a man of furious temper, and when roused his anger was little short of insanity. So, what with his anxiety to get on, and what with his aching foot, and what with the ridiculous figure he was making in the public road, he lost his self-control and fell a-scolding "like a very drab." So fiercely was he belaboring the ass with his staff that for the instant he did not even notice the astounding circumstance of the ass speaking to him with a human voice, but answered back again, as if bound to quarrel with all comers, "I would there were a sword in my hand, for now would I kill thee."

It was but for a moment that a man could be so transported with rage as not to recognize so startling a miracle; and when Balaam recovered himself sufficiently to look up, he saw an object in the highway in whose presence his anger suddenly froze to fear. There stood a mighty angel with a drawn sword in his hand, and the ass had seen it before its master. This sight, of course, brought the man down, and he fell upon his face. Now he began pleading guilty. Now he offered to abandon the whole business, although it had advanced so far, and return directly home. Now he only wished he had never heard of Balak or had anything to do with his offers. But he cannot be let off at this point. God has some work for him to do. He has been pretending to deal in the supernatural; let him try the reality a while. "Go on," says the angel; but as if pointing to the life of falsehood that Balaam had led, he adds, "Only the word that I speak unto thee, that shalt thou speak."

By this time the Hebrew camp has moved down from the eastern heights, and is resting upon one of the broad terraces of the valley of the Jordan. So when Balaam arrives, the king takes him to a good outlook on the hills in the rear, and after preliminary sacrifices bids him do his duty. Now for the curse at last. Now to see that Hebrew power withered at a single stroke. Now shall Balak effect what Og and Sihon both failed to accomplish.

But as Balaam opens his lips, what strange words are those he begins to utter? "How shall I curse," he says—"how shall I curse whom God hath not cursed, and how shall I defy whom God hath not defied?" Balaam is not responsible for that speech, be it right or wrong. A power has seized his utterance which he cannot control. It is another heart, another mind, another will, speaking by his organs, and forcing him to an utterance against which he would fain set his whole soul; and now that the prophetic impulse is upon him, it carries him out upon a current of blessings, pouring down evermore in life and love upon the people whom he came to destroy.

Balak, in alarm, breaks in upon him, and endeavors to change the current by changing place. Come away, he says. Let us go to another hill-top and come at the business from an opposite quarter. So Balaam tries again, and it is just as before. His will is good enough, but he cannot control his own words. Balak begs him to desist. If he cannot curse them, will he not at least refrain from blessing them? But Balaam is no more his own master. As he was not allowed to pronounce the curse, so is he not allowed to remain silent. God has him in hand, and he is but a harp in the grasp of the great Harper. So he pours out benedictions, prophecies of glory, pictures of conquest and revelations of joy. He gets a glimpse even of the great Messiah, and tells what a Star shall rise upon the land where that happy people shall dwell.

The thing has to be given up. Balak's project has as surely failed him as did the projects of Sihon, king of the Amorites, and Og, king of Bashan. Balaam is overmastered, and the curse is turned to a blessing.

At a later day and under more subtle counsel Balak's wishes were in part fulfilled. Num. xxxi. 16 and xxv. 4, 15. When the Hebrews were enticed into sinful intercourse with the Moabites and with their allies the Midianites, there was no further difficulty in bringing them under a curse. And out of that intercourse came a war between Israel and the Midianites in which Balaam perished. Num. xxxi. 8.

Such was this strange character whose figure rises so conspicuously before us in those ancient times—a true prophet only as he was caught in his own net, and compelled to meet the solemn realities to which he had made pretensions; a thoroughly bad man, compelled to act a good part against his own inclinations; a man that had traded in the fame that the God Jehovah had won, and who for his own purposes affected to be his worshiper, but who sold himself to work iniquity, and who perished amid the plots he was laying against the people of the Lord. The prophecies he uttered rank among the sweetest to be found on the page of inspiration; but knowing what was in his heart, we give his fitting epitaph in the words of the apostle: "Though I speak with the tongues of men and of angels, though I have the gift of prophecy and understand all mysteries and all knowledge, and though I have all faith, so that I could remove mountains, and have not charity, I am nothing." 1 Cor. xiii. 1.

LII.

DEATH OF MOSES.

THE children of Israel have lingered long enough on the eastern shore. It is time they passed over and took possession of their inheritance. But before they go Moses must take his leave of them. He has been too well apprised of the destiny awaiting him to be alarmed at the announcement, and yet it is a solemn moment when the words come, "Behold the days approach that thou must die."

Instantly, on the receipt of this message, he sets himself to prepare for the occasion. He maps out the promised land, and assigns to each tribe its inheritance. He appoints Joshua to take his place as leader of the people. He passes through the camp to see that everything is in order; and then, gathering the people about him, he delivers that lengthened valedictory which constitutes our book of Deuteronomy, sings with them a parting hymn, pronounces a benediction upon them tribe by tribe, and so takes his leave.

The circumstances of his death were much like those of Aaron's. Moses, however, takes no companion with him up into the mountain where he is to meet his fate, but goes entirely alone. He marches out of the camp in full strength. One might suppose him taking a walk for his recreation. He does not step as if the weight of an hundred and twenty years were upon him. He ascends those heights to the eastward, on which Balaam just now kindled his altar fires; and seeking out the lofty summit to which God directed him to go, he climbs to the top and prepares to depart.

It is recorded particularly how vigorous the old man was, special mention being made of his good eyesight. And when he stood upon that lofty watch-tower, his clear vision spanned the country round. Yonder, just breaking the edge of the southern horizon, were the outworks and approaches of Mount Hor and Edom. To the east lay the conquered kingdoms of Og and Sihon. Beneath him, in the valley, gleamed the white tents of Israel, and stretching out beyond the Jordan, a picture of matchless beauty, was the object that had so long been his great earthly hope, <u>the promised land</u>.

At such a moment how his own personal history would pass before his mind!—that eventful history the like of which was never else to be written of mortal man. The scenes he had witnessed at the Egyptian court, the quiet life he had led when he kept Raguel's flock, the fierce excitements of the Exodus and the stirring incidents that had attended the journey through the desert,—how would these things throng upon him at such an hour!

That was all past now, and he stood there alone—ready to go, no doubt, yet who could question that he loved the world in which he had dwelt so long, and that his heart clung fondly to the people whom he had borne for forty years upon his bosom? One imagines him lingering tenderly over what he saw at that moment and waiting a little before he would say his last adieu.

Of all the sights that now greeted his enlarged vision, however, we may well judge that the chief which filled his soul was the goodly land which he had so long sought to enter, and which was now to be his people's home. There it lay, bathed in the vivid brightness of that Oriental sunshine, and as he gazed the radiance grew more and more wonderful. Slowly the earthly scene melted into one that was heavenly. Canaan was the material framework in which was set a picture that was spiritual, and the lonely watch-tower where he stood grew populous with the presence of beings whose make was more than mortal. He heard the rustle of wings. He caught glimpses of shining ones about him, and up, as from some unknown depths, there came notes of praise. Indistinct were they at first, and low, as reaching from afar, but rising in a grand crescendo till the anthem shook the solid spheres. Higher still it rose, and deeper rolled. It heaved its mighty billows over his soul. It dashed its living spray beyond the stars. Then how his eyes were opened and what new senses came into play! And yonder stood that majestic Presence a glimpse of whom overwhelmed his mind at Mount Sinai, and the same voice that called to him out of the burning bush called again, saying, "Blessed are the pure in heart, for they shall see God."

On earth it was said, "Moses is dead." God buried him, and no man knoweth of his sepulchre unto this day. It is well. Superstition would have reveled in the possession of such a man's tomb, and relics from his body would have been hawked about the whole world. God forestalled that mischief, and buried him alone.

Moses died three thousand years ago. Since then he has dwelt in the presence of the divine glory, and has been the possessor of all the joy of heaven. The happy portion thus allotted him in the world to which he has gone is the fruit of a certain choice he once made. Heb. xi. 24, 26. He made that choice when he was young. Did he ever regret it? Does he regret it now?

"By faith, Moses, when he was come to years, refused to be called the son of Pharaoh's daughter, choosing rather to suffer affliction with the people of God than to enjoy the pleasures of sin for a season. For he had respect unto the recompense of the reward."

www.ingramcontent.com/pod-product-compliance
Lightning Source LLC
Chambersburg PA
CBHW030115240426
43673CB00041B/1295